A WALKING TOUR IN SOUTHERN FRANCE

A WALKING TOUR OF SOUTHERN FRANCE (1912)

FRANCE

• Cholet

Châtellerault

• Chantannay   • Châteauroux
          • Poitiers
                    • Montmorillon
• Niort

          • Bellac   • Montlucon
• Rochefort
          Limoges•   Clermont-
Cognac • Chalus•   •Excideuil   Ferrand
Angoulême •Mareuil Hautefort
Chalais•   Uzerce• •Ussel   Brioude•
Ribérac•   •Périgueux •Brive Ventadour   Allègre•
                        Aurillac•   Le Puy•
Cadillac•   Sarlat•   •Souillac
          Domme• •Gourdon
Bordeaux•   •   Aumont•
     Cahors•
          •Rodez   Beaucaire•
Nerac•   Tarascon•
     Gaillac•
• Leon   •Eauze   •Albi   Nîmes•
• Hagetmau Toulouse•   Montpellier•   Durance
Bayonne•   •Mielan   Béziers• Agde   Arles• River
     •Tarbes   Carcassonne•

          Foix•
PYRENEES MTS. •Quillan
          Perpignan•

SPAIN   MEDITERRANEAN
          Andorra   SEA

0   25   50   75 100
          Miles

ATLANTIC OCEAN

Leyre R.
Lot River
Garonne River

Allier River
Loire River
Rhône River
Ain River
Isère River

——— 1st portion of walking tour
═══ 2nd portion of walking tour

A WALKING TOUR
IN SOUTHERN FRANCE

Ezra Pound among
the Troubadours

EDITED AND INTRODUCED
BY RICHARD SIEBURTH

A NEW DIRECTIONS BOOK

The epigraph on page vii, from Paul Blackburn's *Proensa: An Anthology of Troubadour Poetry* (Copyright © 1978), is reprinted by permission of the University of California Press.

Previously published works of Ezra Pound are quoted or reprinted in this volume by permission of The Trustees of the Ezra Pound Literary Property Trust and New Directions Publishing Corporation. *The Cantos of Ezra Pound* (Copyright © 1934, 1937, 1940, 1948, 1950, 1956, 1959, 1962, 1963, 1965, 1966, 1968, 1970, 1971 by Ezra Pound; Copyright © 1973, 1986 by The Trustees of the Ezra Pound Literary Property Trust). *Personae* (Copyright © 1926, 1935, 1971 by Ezra Pound). "Fragment 4B" of Canto 4 (Copyright © 1984 by the Trustees of the Ezra Pound Literary Property Trust).

Manufactured in the United States of America
New Directions Books are published on acid-free paper.
First published clothbound in 1992
Published simultaneously in Canada by Penguin Books Canada Limited

Library of Congress Cataloging in Publication Data

Pound, Ezra, 1885–1972.
    A walking tour in Southern France / Ezra Pound ; edited and
introduced by Richard Sieburth.
      p. cm.
    ISBN 0-8112-1223-8
    1. Pound, Ezra, 1885–1972—Journeys—France, Southern. 2. France,
Southern—Description and travel. 3. Poets, American—20th century—
Diaries. 4. Literary landmarks—France, Southern. 5. Walking—
France, Southern. 6. Troubadours. I. Sieburth, Richard.
II. Title.
PS3531.082Z477   1992
818'.5203—dc20
[B]   92–19890
                                           CIP

New Directions Books are published for James Laughlin
by New Directions Publishing Corporation,
80 Eighth Avenue, New York 10011

Contents

Introduction

"To Set Here the Roads of France"

Ab l'alen tir vas me l'aire
qu'ieu sen venir de Proensa
tot quant es de lai m'agensa
        Peire Vidal

I suck deep in air come from Provence to here.
All things from there so please me.
        Paul Blackburn

Rummaging among his papers at Brunnenburg in 1958, shoring fragments against ruin, Ezra Pound came across a cache of writings nearly half a century old—a series of small French school notebooks filled with his observations of the troubadour landscape of southern France as seen on foot in the summer of 1912. The discovery of these notebooks, his daughter Mary recalls, occasioned a moment of hope at the castle, a brief gleam of remembered beauty amid the gathering silence and depression. Sifting through his memorabilia, Pound had also turned up an ancient snapshot of his Aunt Frank perched on a mule in Tangiers in 1898—a memento of his first Grand Tour of Europe at age twelve which he now tacked up over the door to his study in homage to the portly Victorian globetrotter who had initiated him into a lifetime of restless wanderings. His young disciple and amanuensis, Marcella Spann, was put to work making a fair copy of the yellowing sheaf of materials that had acquired the manuscript title *Walking Tour 1912*, but after a few pages of transcription the entire initiative ground to a halt, apparently a casualty of Pound's own flagging spans of will and attention ("And I am not a demi-god, / I cannot make it cohere"). All that remains of the book he hoped to quarry from the lode of his 1912 walking tour are a few scattered outcroppings of southern French place-names amid the late paradisal landscapes of *Thrones*, and this final injunction to remembrance at the close of *Drafts and Fragments:* "to set here the roads of France."

From Brunnenburg, the *Walking Tour* eventually traveled with the rest of the Pound archives to the Beinecke Library in the late '70s, where Donald Gallup, then curator of the collection of American literature at Yale, made another stab at its transcription before giving up after some twenty pages. And no wonder, for the manuscript had by this point become a virtually impenetrable jumble: only three of the original autograph notebooks (totaling about 100 pages) still survived intact, while the remaining 160 pages consisted of detached sheets interleaved with occasional pieces of hotel stationery, scraps of research notes from the Bibliothèque Nationale, and snippets of Chinese destined for late *Cantos*—the entire packet arranged in no discernible sequence and arbitrarily divided up into three archival folders. What's more, the handwritten state of these materials—page after tiny page covered with a traveler's hasty scrawl—was enough to make the most patient of paleographers blanch.

When it finally came this editor's turn to try his hand at decipherment, it rapidly became clear that faced with a text this recalcitrant to philology, the only path of interpretation lay through the roads of France. Armed with detailed Michelin maps and with the guidebooks Pound had himself consulted (Baedeker's 1907 *Southern France*, the 1877 Guide Joanne to the Pyrenees, and Justin Smith's 1898 *Troubadours at Home*), he retraced the itinerary of that summer of 1912, discovering in the process that in almost every case the actual details of observed geography clarified the most puzzling cruxes of the manuscript. This "pedestrian" method of scholarship (as Donald Davie has called it), which involves shuttling back and forth between the realm of real topographical referents and the domain of written signifiers, confutes most modern theories of textuality.[1] But in the case of Pound's *Walking Tour*, the text only began to take on a legible face when correlated with the close inspection of place. What this peripatetic editing process eventually (and quite unexpectedly) revealed was a remarkably readable account of a journey in search of the vanished voices of Provence that at the same time chronicled Pound's gradual discovery of himself as a modernist poet among the landscapes of southern France.

Pound's fascination with the troubadours reached back to his university days: he studied Provençal with William P. Shepard as an undergraduate at Hamilton College in 1904–05 and pursued his training in romance philology on the graduate level under Hugo Rennert at the University of Pennsylvania the following year.[2] Despite a 1906 summer fellowship to do research in Spain on a doctoral dissertation that was to have analyzed the role of the *gracioso* in the plays of Lope de Vega, Pound never completed his Ph.D. in Romanics at Penn. His disastrous experience as an assistant professor of Romance Languages at Wabash College in Crawfordsville, Indiana, in 1907–08 sealed his contempt for academia and eventually landed him in Venice later that year, where he published his first book of poems, *A Lume Spento*, which contained, among other Pre-Raphaelite anachronisms, his earliest adaptations of troubadour poetry.

Pound's subsequent volumes of verse—*Personae* (1909), *Exultations* (1909), *Provença* (1910), *Canzoni* (1911)—continued this series of experiments in transforming romance philology into contemporary poetry, largely through the medium of translation or Browningesque monologues in the personae of such figures as Bertran de Born, Peire Vidal, or Arnaut de Mareuil. To the extent that both of these modes hinged on mimetic feats of identification—the miming of rhyme and meter in the case of translation, the impersonation of voice in the case of dramatic monologue—they tended to efface the distance between self and other, English and Provençal, medieval and modern, thus prefiguring Pound's later axiom that "all ages are contemporaneous." At the same time, however, his early verse still remained very much under the sway of a post-romantic exoticism that prized Provence not as a potential version of the present, but rather as a secret Yeatsian land whose very glamor (heightened by supererogatory cedilla) depended on its remoteness and whose hieratic rites of love could only be intimated by negation:

> 'Tis not a game that plays at mates and mating,
> Provençe knew;
> 'Tis not a game of barter, lands and houses,
> Provençe knew.
> We who are wise beyond your dream of wisdom,
> Drink our immortal moments; we "pass through."
> We have gone forth beyond your bond and borders,
> Provençe knew . . .

Though he was later to reject most of his early verse as "stale creampuffs," these initial reworkings of troubadour poetry nonetheless established the fundamental poles of Pound's topos of Provence—a site situated somewhere between the oral and the written, between exultation and elegy, between immediacy and loss.

Alongside these poetic forays into the eros and ethos of Provence, Pound continued to pursue his scholarly investigations into the historical and cultural contexts of troubadour song. In late 1909, he offered a "Course of Lectures on Medieval Literature" at the Polytechnic Institute of London; revised and expanded, these essays on Arnaut Daniel, the troubadours of "Proença," Cavalcanti, Dante, and Villon were published the following year as *The Spirit of Romance*, Pound's first major attempt to define the canon of his own poetic tradition to the broader public. In early 1911, he embarked on an edition of *The Canzoni of Arnaut Daniel*, conceived as a companion volume to his forthcoming *Sonnets and Ballate of Guido Cavalcanti* (1912). Ten translations of Arnaut's cansos accompanied by erudite analyses of *il miglior fabbro*'s art of rhyme, rhythm, and "tone-leading" appeared in a series of essays that ran in *The New Age* over the winter of 1911–12, but Pound's projected edition of the troubadour never materialized: a victim of the vagaries of midwestern American publishing, the project would have to wait till 1920 to appear in abbreviated form as a chapter of *Instigations*.[3]

Pound's particular attentiveness to Arnaut Daniel's crafting of *motz el son* ("the strict relation of word and tune") led him to the Ambrosian Library in Milan in the spring of 1911, where he had photographs made of the Ms R71 superiore—the sole manuscript containing the musical notation for two of Arnaut's poems (*"Chansson doil mot"* and *"Lo ferm voler"*). His research into troubadour melopoeia had in large part been stimulated by his collaboration with the German-born pianist and composer Walter Morse Rummel, grandson of the American inventor of telegraph code and member of Debussy's Parisian coterie. Pound shared Rummel's fashionable Passy flat at 92 rue Raynouard from March through May of 1911 and together the two worked out settings of three lyrics from *Canzoni*—published later that year in London as *Three Songs of Ezra Pound for a Voice with Instrumental Accompaniment*. During this same Paris stay, Pound also spent considerable time at the Bibliothèque Nationale copying out music from Provençal *chansonniers:* his notebooks of the period show him trying to transcode the blocky geometries of the medieval parchments into modern musical notation—scribal semiotics in the service of voice.[4] All these archival labors would bear fruit the following year when Pound again returned to Paris to resume work with Rummel. Over the course of the spring and summer of 1912, the composer devised settings for Pound's English versions of nine troubadour songs, published bilingually the following year under the title *Hesternae Rosae, Serta II, Neuf Chansons de Troubadours des XIIième et XIIIième Siècles*.[5]

Despite the rather *fin-de-siècle* redolence of these "Roses of Yesteryear," the melopoeia Pound was learning to discern in Arnaut Daniel's songs had little to do with the indefinite symbolist condition of music.[6] Under the tutelage of Ford Madox Ford (who had mercilessly ridiculed the "tertiary archaisms" of his 1911 *Canzoni*), Pound's poetics were undergoing a slow sea-change from the spirit of romance into something he was now beginning to call "experiments in modernity," enacted in an idiom "austere, direct, free from emotional slither" (LE, 12). The catchwords of this new aesthetic—"precision," "accuracy of statement," "objectivity"—derived from Ford's theoretical distillations of the prose praxis of the 19th-century realist novel, grounded in a mystique of scientific exactitude. By late 1911, therefore, even Arnaut's music (traditionally the least referential of the arts) was becoming for Pound a mimetic measure of the "precision of observation and reference" with which the troubadour had registered the details of his world. Whereas "long after him the poets of the North babbled of gardens where 'three birds sang on every bough' and where other things and creatures behaved as in nature they do not behave," Pound was now convinced that the same "fineness of Arnaut's senses which made him chary of his rhymes, impatient of tunes that

would have distorted his language, fastidious of redundance, made him likewise accurate in his observation of Nature" (SP, 27). Arnaut's "explicit ren-
dering, be it of external nature, or of emotion," Pound wrote in February
1912, provided "testimony of the eyewitness" (LE, 11). Three months later
he was off to the Continent to test his theories against the actual landscapes of
Provence.

He prepared for his periplus by studying *Troubadours at Home*, Dartmouth
professor Justin Smith's two-volume account of his travels through southern
France in 1895 and 1898.[7] Lavishly illustrated with photographs, the book
provided the general public with an exotic tapestry of travelogue, scholarly
excursus, and historical romance—pre-Raphaelite medievalism brought up to
date by the camera and the motorcar. Preferring to consult the original
source-material on the troubadours' lives rather than rely on Smith's *vies
romancées*, Pound spent early May in Paris reading the Provençal *vidas* and
razos conserved as Ms. 854 (siglum I) and Ms. 12373 (siglum K) at the Bibliothèque Nationale. Even though the French scholar Gaston Paris had de-
cisively demonstrated in 1893 that these biographies of the troubadours were
for the most part a tissue of fictions, Pound was still enough of a positivist to
take them as evidential fact.[8] What above all drew him to these *vidas*, however, was their elliptical compaction of information—entire poetic careers
epitomized by a few dramatic gists. Ancestors of the Italian novellas of the
Renaissance (and of the modern short story), these brief lives indicated a
minimalist alternative to the girth of the 19th-century historical or psycho-
logical novel. Translated and summarized in Pound's 1913 "Troubadours:
Their Sorts and Conditions" (see APP 1), the spare, paratactic narratives of
the *vidas* point unmistakably ahead to the modernist historiography and portraiture of the *Cantos*.
Having completed his preliminary background research and acquired a
membership in the Touring Club de France, Pound set forth for the Midi in
late May. His first stop was Poitiers, site of the court of the first known
troubadour, William IX, and "mother city" of Provençal song. From Poitiers,
he proceeded by rail to Angoulême, before striking out on foot to Chalais,
Ribérac (birthplace of Arnaut Daniel), Mareuil (the castle of the "lesser Arnaut"), Périgueux, Hautefort (Bertran de Born's fortress), Excideuil (home of
Giraut de Borneil), and Chalus (site of the slaying of Richard Coeur de Lion).
After a fortnight on the road—over the course of which he had walked some
225 kilometers, staying mostly at country inns—Pound arrived by train at
Limoges around June 7, only to learn from letters awaiting him at *poste restante*
that Margaret Cravens, the young American patroness whom he had been
cultivating (and some hinted, emotionally leading on) that spring in Paris, had
shot herself shortly after his departure for the South. He returned posthaste
to Paris, where he tried to assuage her distraught American aunt who had in

the meantime disembarked in the wake of the tragedy.[9] Veering between bouts of depression and bursts of confidence, he spent most of June at Rummel's Passy flat correcting the proofs of his most recent volume of verse, *Ripostes*, continuing work at the Bibliothèque Nationale, hosting Hilda Doolittle and Richard Aldington (another emotional imbroglio), and revising the notes of his walking tour into two chapters that he sent off to his fiancée Dorothy Shakespear as the first installment of his new "opus 411."[10]

By June 27 he was on the road again. From Uzerche, he moved south to Brive and Souillac, and walked through the valley of the Dordogne to Sarlat, Domme, and then down to Gourdon. There he caught a train to Cahors and Rodez, whence he set off on foot for Albi and Toulouse, capital city of troubadour poetry. After traveling on by rail to Foix, he hiked through the Pyrenees to Axat, took a train to Carcassonne and Narbonne and then walked to Béziers and Agde along the Languedoc coast. After resting up for a week in Arles, Nîmes, and Beaucaire, he then trekked through the mountains of the Auvergne, stopping at Allègre and Chaise-Dieu before finally reaching Clermont-Ferrand on July 19. In the space of a little more than three weeks, he had covered about a thousand kilometers of the Midi, half of them on foot. Once back in Paris, he began recasting his travel notes for the "opus" that had by now acquired the title of *Gironde* (after the river that flowed through Toulouse). By the end of July, he was proudly writing Dorothy from Paris that he had already finished half the book.

Over the next two months in London, Pound continued work on the project, trying to hone his prose by the reading of Montaigne, Flaubert, and Turgenev. He announced to his Aunt Frank that the soon to be published volume was intended as a gesture of gratitude for the two tours of Europe she had taken him on as an adolescent.[11] He showed eighty pages of the nearly completed manuscript to Ford Madox Ford, who brutally informed him that its prose was as bad as Robert Louis Stevenson's jejune account of his *Travels with a Donkey in the Cévennes* (1879). Disheartened, Pound wrote Dorothy in late September, "I've hung about the 1st 1/3 of *Gironde* on my west wall as a sign that I'm dam'd if I bother much more with revising it."[12] Thereafter the book apparently withered on the vine. Pound, at any rate, was already beginning to move in other directions. Freshly appointed foreign editor of Chicago's *Poetry* magazine, his energies were now increasingly devoted to establishing his reputation as the modernist mover behind the newly founded school of Imagism. In addition, "Patria Mia," a series of essays on America based on his brief return stateside in late 1910, was appearing in *The New Age*—and for a brief moment he thought he might salvage *Gironde* by printing it with these American notes as a diptych entitled *Studies in Medievalism Past and Present* (the juxtaposition turning on the metaphor of two "medieval" cultures emerging from the Dark Ages and poised on the brink of renaissance).[13] The last one hears of *Gironde* is in a letter of the following spring

where Pound half-heartedly wonders whether the manuscript could be ped-
dled to an American publisher: "I've got a damn rotten prose thing, neither
fish nor feather, a walk in the troubadour country with notes on the troubadour lives etc. Awful hash. *Harzreise* with Heine left out, sort of mud-
dle . . . Prose has commercial value, increasing according to its worse-
ness."[14]

The typescript of *Gironde* having vanished, one can only surmise what kind
of book it might have formed. Judging from various allusions in his corre-
spondence with Dorothy, Pound had apparently attempted to intersperse the
narrative of his walking tour with excerpts from the troubadour *vidas* and
translations of their poems, while mixing in occasional prose soliloquies and
critical divagations on the craft and context of Provençal song (two surviving
chapters destined for *Gironde* may be found at the end of this volume). Presumably intended as an assemblage of historical documents, illustrative quo-
tations, and vignettes of a poet's voyage through time and space (a hint of the
Cantos to come?), *Gironde* seems to have been modeled on the open form of the
Montaignian essay (the perfect vehicle for registering the gait of a consciousness in motion) and on the impressionistic polyphonies of romantic travel
writing (hence the allusion to Heine's *Harzreise*). If Pound was unable to make
this patchwork of moods and materials cohere, it was largely because (as Ford
immediately discerned) he was completely out of his depth when it came to
writing narrative prose ("As an artist I dislike prose," he confessed in 1911.
"Writing prose is an art, but it is not my art"). Under contract from Stephen
Swift & Co. to receive £100 per year advance royalties against all future
works and seriously in need of funds after the suicide of his patroness Margaret Cravens, Pound had in all likelihood undertaken *Gironde* as a commercial
venture. When Swift went bankrupt in November 1912, there was simply no
more financial incentive to complete a project whose style, shape, and audience continued to elude him. In the end, the sole published writings to
emerge from his travels in southern France proved to be a group of 1915
poems—"Provencia Deserta," "The Gypsy," and "Near Perigord" (see APP
2). As for the ill-starred *Gironde*, it now only exists as a phantom item in the
Borgesian bibliography of Pound's lost or unwritten books.
    Although of uneven literary quality, the surviving first draft notes of the
journey that was to have provided the narrative backbone of *Gironde* nonetheless offer a rare portrait of Pound at a decisive turning point in his career—age
twenty-six, no longer the archaizing minstrel of *Canzoni* but not quite yet
fully at home in the modernist esthetic (the so-called "School of Images")
announced in the postface to *Ripostes*. From the very first pages of his manuscript, Pound admits to hesitating between two opposite models of travel
writing—on the one hand, the "voyage of sentiment" (in which the *dépayse-
ment* of foreign parts serves as a stimulus to "strange and exquisite emotions"),

and on the other hand, the "realist" method of presentation, based on the "scientific" registering of observed fact and sensation. This hesitation informs his entire periplus through Provence: wavering between the subjective and the objective, between empathy and impersonality, between straightforward narrative prose and lyric epiphany, the manuscript is not just the record of a search for the vestiges of troubadour culture: it is also (as Pound later described *Personae*) a "search for 'sincere self-expression'" among a series of styles and identities provisionally assumed by a sensibility intent on experiencing its own displacements.

The personae Pound adopts in his *Walking Tour* are various, their moods swinging from professorial dyspepsia to garrulous bonhomie, from schoolboy ebullience to wistful melancholia. All these literary masks are in a sense a measure of what he at one point in his manuscript refers to as "this modern, false modern self-consciousness." Although it is the only extended first-person narrative Pound ever wrote (with the exception of his brief 1923 experiment in parodic self-portraiture, *Indiscretions*), this self-consciousness effectively inhibits the autobiographical dimensions one might have expected of such a text. Indeed, apart from a passing allusion to "false friends and lying reviewers" and a brief admission to the effect that "I have made horrible mistakes, I have lived thru horrible things—but horrible," the manuscript makes no reference to the complex web of personal entanglements and betrayals that attended its writing—notably, Pound's fatally equivocal dealings with Margaret Cravens, not to mention his still ambivalent courtship of Dorothy Shakespear or ongoing intimacies with ex-fiancées Mary Moore and Hilda Doolittle.

This intricate constellation of liaisons (whose erotics, Pound hinted in his 1912 essay "Psychology and Troubadours," derived from the sublimation of sexuality into a "cult of Amor" intensified by an ascetic discipline of deferral and delay) figures only indirectly in the *Walking Tour*, primarily through metaphorical association with Bertran de Born's "*Dompna pois de me no'us chal*" ["Lady, since you care nothing for me"], a *sirventes* centered around the enigmatic figure of a *dompna soiseubuda* or "composite lady" whose ideal beauty is fabricated out of the fragmentary features of the fairest women of Provence—"Of Anhes, her hair gold as Ysolt's; of Cembelins, the expression of her eyes; of Aelis, her easy speech, of the Viscountess of Chales, her throat and her two hands" (SOR, 47). Having earlier adapted this *blason* of female attributes in *A Lume Spento* under the title "Na Audiart," Pound now set out to verify its topographical references against the actual sites in the Limousin and Périgord mentioned in the Bertran's poem.

He was testing a rather daring (if unfounded) theory about the text, namely, that the erotic riddle of the *dompna soiseubuda* in fact veiled Bertran's military designs on the network of castles occupied by each of the ladies whose charms he celebrated—the troubadour language of love merely masking a power play against male rivals for the strategic control of territory. As he inspected the strongholds of Chalais and Hautefort or explored the hills to the east of Périgueux, Pound sought to decipher the hidden political meanings of Bertran's poem by directly applying the techniques of textual hermeneutics to a reading of landscape. His description of the terrain in the *Walking Tour* as a chessboard of strategic possibilities transforms the local geography into a topographical allegory of Bertran de Born's embattled psyche—castles perched high on the lookout for attackers, towers stiffened against the hostile plain, dark valleys lurking in potential ambush. Though convinced this mapping of topographical data followed the scientific procedures of romance philology, Pound was in fact unconsciously projecting his own private scenarios of phallic beleaguerment and grandeur onto the landscape of his troubadour alter-ego. By 1915, when he again returned to the riddles of Bertran de Born's *sirventes* in the poem "Near Perigord," Pound had considerably revised his earlier positivistic assumptions about the feasibility of reconstructing the actual historical facts of the troubadour's turbulent *vida* from the local lay of the land. The poem concludes that our partial vision of the past may be (like the "composite lady" herself) nothing more than an unstable narcissistic projection—"And all the rest of her a shifting change, / A broken bundle of mirrors . . . !"

At the outset of his 1912 walking tour, however, Pound was still proceeding on the belief that the referential ground of troubadour song might be recovered through the simple exercise of "inspective energy." Ambling down the valley of the Dronne near Arnaut Daniel's birthplace at Ribérac, he verified the vernal vegetation of the countryside against vocabulary of the poet's *cansos*. Observing the rhythm of "cusps & hills, of prospects opened & shut" as the road climbed northward toward Mareuil, he wondered whether the structure of Arnaut's sestinas might not derive from patterns of recurrence in the local terrain. Having fought the wind and rain through the greater part of his journey, he reflected that he now "found a deal more force in certain lines & stanzas than I had ever expected . . . if we consider them as sung by men to whom the condition of the weather was a necessary concomitant of every action & enjoyment . . . the prelude of weather in nearly every canzon becomes self evident, it is the actual reflection." (Three decades later, exposed to the elements at Pisa, the full force of these observations would hit home.)

But despite the insights gathered along the road into the nomadic existence of the troubadours (the prime features of which seemed to him the utter boredom of castle life and the extreme arduousness of travel), Pound's account of his walking tour vacillates between a confidence that the mysteries of Provençal song might be philologically or imaginatively recovered and an elegiac awareness that the world he is seeking to resurrect is irrevocably lost, accessible only as trace or ruin—that it may be (as he notes at one point in his manuscript) no more than a land "thick with ghosts" through which he travels like some belated "dealer in garments of the dead." Although this *nekuia* is occasionally relieved by glimpses into rural customs or urban festivals—such as the Feast of the Trinity in Périgueux or St. John's Eve at Gourdon—whose archaic communal rites of fertility seemed to bear irrefutable witness to the survival of the pagan folk traditions at the root of Provençal poetry, Pound's narrative (at least in its early segments) nonetheless skirts the risk of falling into the solipsistic and spectral "phantastikon" (as he termed it) that had afflicted much of his early *fin-de-siècle* poetry and that would continue to haunt the first versions of his *Cantos:* "Ghosts move about me / Patched with histories . . ."[15]

"I had set out upon this book with numerous ideas, but the road had cured me of them," Pound writes at the outset of the second portion of his journey. "There is this difference, I think between a townsman & a man doing something or going somewhere in the open, namely that the townsman has his head full of abstractions. The man in the open has his mind full of objects." Moving southward at a considerable clip through the Dordogne, the Quercy, and down into the Pyrenees and the Languedoc, Pound jettisoned the scholarly baggage that he had tried to bring to bear on the sites visited during the first leg of his trip and began concentrating on the immediacies of physical sensation—the steady rhythm of walking punctuated by the pleasures of the table (as he later recalled his journey in *Guide to Kulchur:* "In every town a romanesque church or château. No place to stay for any time, but food every ten miles or fifteen or twenty. When I say food, I mean food. . . . Le Voyage Gastronomique is a French paideuma"). Above all, he increasingly gave his eye over to objects chanced upon along the way, trying to seize the *genius loci* not through the lens of textual or historical reminiscence but in the sheer *visibilia* of place. As he essayed this new-found discipline of seeing (Rilke's *Augenwerk*) on the landscapes and townscapes of southern France, Pound gradually managed to transform his eye into a modernist organ of phanopoeia through the unlikely medium of descriptive travel prose.

Much as Wordsworth's *Descriptive Sketches* announce *The Prelude,* so the imagistic notations of place scattered throughout the *Walking Tour* unmistakably prepare the palette for the *Cantos.* To choose only one example among many, Pound's observation of the iambic play of light and water on the river Dordogne—"a band of bluish metal with rippled chevrons in the shallows"—displays a precision of painterly detail nowhere evident in his earlier writings; it needs only the inflection of a few spondees to acquire the characteristic prosodic signature of the *Cantos:* "a wine-red glow in the shallows, / a tin flash in the sun-dazzle" (2/7). This kind of attention to the visual surface of landscape, as Tony Tanner has argued, is a characteristic trait of American romanticism (as opposed to the auditory depth and resonance with

nature sought after by the European romantics).[16] Pound's transit through
the Midi is, in this respect, a typically American pilgrimage, the rapid trajec-
tory through space of an Emersonian "transparent eyeball" ("I am nothing; I
see all") intent primarily on registering its fleeting visual impressions of the
external scene. The very ocularity of Pound's relation to the mobile theater of
landscape implies a severance of subject and object, a gap between eye and
thing, self and other—indeed, the solitude of the *Walking Tour* is virtually
unrelieved by any significant human encounter. But it is precisely this emotional and pictorial remove that Pound the Imagist is after: unwittingly para-
phrasing Emerson's wonder at the "cool disengaged air of natural objects," he
describes Poitiers, for example, as a place filled with things that "stand in an
air cool & exquisite & impersonal"—things, in short, that are remarkable for
simply being there, at a distance.

Pound's excursion through southern France thus has little to do with the
Wordsworthian marriage of Imagination and Nature. Indeed Nature, dis-
missed as mere "scenery," is conspicuously absent from the narrative:
Pound's roving eye is only drawn to that already aestheticized (and semi-
otized) arrangement of place into legible contour which he calls "landscape"—
a field of visual particulars seized not as ineffable totality but as a sequence of
detached details whose fragmentation observes the same erotic scenario as the
fetishized attributes of Bertran de Born's "composite lady." Dissociated into a
virtually free-floating pattern of discrete traits, the body of landscape can
thereby be recomposed at will—whether by metaphorical superposition (the
mountains of the Pyrenees overlaid with the mist of Ming landscape painting,
the towers of Périgueux rhymed with the skyscrapers of New York) or by
metonymical juxtaposition (the swift cuts from place to place or name to name
creating a kaleidoscopic montage of topographical features). In "The Alche-
mist," a 1912 poem inspired by his walking tour, Pound transmutes a catalogue of the fairest women of Provence (culled from the troubadour *vidas*) into
a syncretic landscape whose features are at once Ovidian, Dantescan, Provençal, and American—the incantatory act of naming mapping out a visionary
geography of desire:

> Saîl of Claustra, Aelis, Azalais,
> As you move among the bright trees;
> As your voices, under the larches of Paradise
> Make a clear sound,
> Saîl of Claustra, Aelis, Azalais,
> Raimona, Tibors, Berangèrë,
> 'Neath the dark gleam of the sky;
> Under night, the peacock-throated,
> Bring the saffron-coloured shell,
> Bring the red gold of the maple,

> Bring the light of the birch tree in autumn
> Mirals, Cembelins, Audiarda,
>> Remember this fire. [17]

Perceived "ply over ply" or as "planes in relation," any locus can therefore potentially become an omphalos, a site of convergence. "Greece & Orient in Provence," Pound elliptically observes toward the end of his journey, already constructing the kind of ideogram of time and space that would provide the central structural device of the *Cantos*.

Three years later, as he began seriously casting around for the eventual shape of his long poem to come, Pound returned to the poetics of place first adumbrated over the course of his 1912 walking tour. A preparatory fragment of Canto 4 composed around 1915 and entitled "What's poetry" creates a composite topos of Provence, Venice, and Spain through the intersplicing of site and citation:

> There is a castle set,
> The Auvezere, or its Dordoigne, chalk white and whiteish blue,
> Or Golding writes "That night, the Loredan"
> And the blue-black of Venice fills my mind
> And the gilt rafters of the first floor rooms
>> Show there above me all a-red, ablaze,
> "I knew it first, and it was such a year,
> "When first I knew it there was such an air."
> Or "This night it will happen." "Further on."
> Or "Down you go, a mile from Angouleme
> And in an open field there are three steps
> Grey stone, they wait, there is no yard behind them,
> Only the stone piers that have held a gate."
> Or "The red poppies seem to swim in glass"
> That's Spain, your dusty France
>> holds half the colour back,
> Your temperate eyes. . . .
>> "Arles gray, what gray?"
> "The church of St Trophime." [18]

A number of these notations already figure in the *Walking Tour;* for example, the "stone piers" south of Angoulême are described in 1912 as "a little style—formal entrance to nowhere, unless it is a park that shows the wet reach of land southward & all Angoulême in retrospect." When this passage was revised for publication as part of the "Fourth Canto" in 1919, its geography was reconfigured into an ideogram of China, Venice, and Provence. The observed details of place remain intact, but are now divorced from any explicit geographical referent or speaker—a symbolist strategy of signifiers opening out onto empty (or absconded) signifieds:

> Smoke hangs on the stream,
> The peach-trees shed bright leaves in the water,
> Sound drifts in the evening haze,
>   The bark scrapes at the ford,
> Gilt rafters above black water,
>   Three steps in an open field,
> Gray stone-posts leading . . .

Three steps, three suspension points leading . . . nowhere. Utopos.

The initial versions of Cantos 1 through 3, the so-called "Three Cantos" first published in *Poetry* in 1917, also draw substantially (and often verbatim) from the *Walking Tour*. Experimentally testing his own firsthand investigations into troubadour sites and *vidas* against Browning's imaginative reconstruction of the life and times of the poet Sordello, Pound returns to Arles, Beaucaire, Gourdon, and the valley of the Dordogne to establish the historical and topographical ground for a modern poetics more adequate to the epic resurrection of the past as *"our* life, your life, my life, extended."[19] In the process, he retrospectively recomposes the places of Provence into a theophanic landscape that ranges encyclopedically in space and time from ancient Greece, Rome, and China through Renaissance Spain and Italy to the present. The results are sometimes even more awkward than the "Wordsworthian, false-pastoral manner" that he so disparagingly dismisses over the course of these Ur-Cantos: "Dordoigne! When I was there, / There came a centaur, spying the land, / And there were nymphs behind him."

Although this kind of neoclassical pastiche substantially disappears from the final revised versions of these Cantos, Pound was obviously casting about for metaphors or myths to convey the visionary intensity of the epiphanies he seems to have undergone, alone in the open for the first time in his life, on the roads of France. The very climate of the place, he later wrote, encouraged one to leave "his nerve-set open" so that the "senses at first seem to project for a few yards beyond the body" (LE, 152). Another unpublished draft of the early Cantos explicitly alludes to these visions:

>   But your visions,
> Your finest visions are half from fever,
> you've admitted it.
>
>   . . .
>
> No. more than half of them when I was hale,
> afoot upon the roads. hearty with walking.
> I'll not tie all thought upon my nether vitals.[20]

This fragment contrasts the feverish domain of libidinally induced hallucination (or "phantastikon") with the pellucid visionary state generated by the Yogic techniques of erotic sublimation hinted at in the 1912 essay "Psychology and Troubadours"—"where the ecstasy is not a whirl or a madness of the senses, but a glow arising from the exact nature of the perception" and where the purified vision of the Lady acts as the medium for a heightened reverence for the inscape of the natural world (SOR, 91).

This quality of attention informs what is perhaps the finest piece of writing to have emerged from Pound's perambulations along the roads of France. First published in 1925 in Robert McAlmon's *Contact Collection of Contemporary Writers* (whose contributors included Djuna Barnes, Ernest Hemingway, H.D., James Joyce, Gertrude Stein, and William Carlos Williams), Canto 20 was submitted by Pound to this avant-garde anthology as a showcase version of pastoral at once medieval and high modernist. Though never explicitly identified, the landscape of this Canto is suffused by the sensorium of Arnaut Daniel's *cansos*,[21] conveyed in cadences as unobtrusive as prose:

> Wind over the olive trees, ranunculae ordered,
> By the clear edge of the rocks
> The water runs, and the wind scented with pine
> And with hay-fields under sun-swath.

The subtle use of deictics (demonstrative adjectives, adverbs of place) manages to point outside the text to some referential bedrock of the real, while at the same time never quite disclosing its actual site:

> You would be happy for the smell of that place
> And never tired of being there, either alone
> Or accompanied.

An immediacy of sensed presence (sight, smell) that suddenly gives way to the aural apprehension of utter distance, a Keatsian or Mallarmean music of absence:

> Sound: as of the nightingale too far off to be heard.

Followed by a swift cut to three Italian painters who bodied forth the radiant Renaissance image of Venus:

> Sandro, and Boccata, and Jacopo Sellaio;

And then eventually back to the elemental *Dasein* of place—air, fire, earth, water:

> Air moving under the boughs,
> The cedars there in the sun,
> Hay new cut on hill slope,
> And the water there in the cut
> Between the two lower meadows; sound,
> The sound, as I have said, a nightingale
> Too far off to be heard.

Ending with a luminous epiphany of the goddess of Love, pivoting on Arnaut's Provençal verb for dazzled vision:

> And the light falls, *remir*
> from her breast to thighs.

Although alluded to throughout the *Cantos* (particularly in the "Pisans"), these ecstatic glimpses of the goddess remain relatively elusive within the manuscript of the *Walking Tour:* such moments tend to be hermetically guarded in Pound's private arcanum. One particular epiphanic instant, however, stands out on the final pages of his narrative. Trekking through the mountains of the Auvergne, Pound came upon the small town of Allègre, site of the impressive ruin of a hilltop medieval fortress whose two towers, connected by a thin bridge of machicolated stonework, stood against the sky like a huge portal opening out onto the wide expanse of landscape below. Looking out at the prospect, hearing (or imagining?) the music of Peire d'Auvergne's famous song to the nightingale (*"Rossinhol al seu repaire"*), Pound carefully noted down the exact time and place (July 16, 4:04 P.M.) of this moment of exaltation, commenting in rather Yeatsian prose: "now should I be finally equipped for the indicting of true pastorals."

Reading through the yellowed notes of his walking tour in the Alpine setting of Brunnenburg nearly half a century later, Pound suddenly remembered this surge of elation at Allègre (the very name of the place means joy). Peire d'Auvergne's nightingales have been transformed into Bernart de Ventadorn's Icarian larks (*"Quant ieu vey la lauzeta mover / De joi sas alas contral ray"*), but the great ruined portal of Allègre still stands there on the very last page of the *Cantos*, now in the mind indestructible, gateway into a paradise whose locus is simply *here:*

> or a field of larks at Allègre,
>   "es laissa cader"
> so high toward the sun and then falling,
>   "de joi sas alas"
> to set here the roads of France.

A NOTE ON THE TEXT

The manuscript of the *Walking Tour* is preserved in folders 3475 through 3477 of the Ezra Pound Archive at the Beinecke Rare Book and Manuscript Library, Yale University. In order to avoid cluttering the text with editorial brackets, Pound's erratic spellings of place-names have been silently corrected and his frequent shorthand abbreviations of proper names and geographic sites emended.

ABBREVIATIONS

The following abbreviations are used for the standard editions of Pound's works, all published by New Directions:

CEP	*Collected Early Poems*
LE	*Literary Essays*
P	*Personae* (revised edition)
SP	*Selected Prose*
SOR	*The Spirit of Romance*
T	*Translations*

The Cantos are cited from the newly repaginated 11th printing (1989), with Canto number followed by the page (e.g., 20/90). APP 1 and APP 2 refer to the appendixes to this present volume.

ACKNOWLEDGMENTS

I would like to thank James Laughlin who made this project possible in the first place. Mary de Rachewiltz provided valuable help in the haruspication of Pound's handwriting. The postcards from the Pounds' 1919 walking tour in southern France that illustrate this edition were kindly provided by Omar Pound. Pat Willis of the Beinecke Library facilitated access to the Pound Archive. Mary Helen McMurran proved an ideal research assistant; Karen Duys came to the rescue on some of the Provençal. A Research Challenge Grant from NYU made travel possible to southern France, where I managed to keep my eye on the road thanks to J., my navigatrix, to whom this edition is dedicated.

A WALKING TOUR IN SOUTHERN FRANCE

Poitiers and Angoulême

Pound set off for the South of France on May 27, traveling by train from Paris to Poitiers. "Mother city" of Provençal poetry and home of the earliest known troubadour, Guillaume IX, who "had brought the song up out of Spain / With the singers and viels" (8/32), Poitiers would later become one of the "sacred places" (as Hugh Kenner has called them) of the *Cantos*. Pound returned to the city in the summer of 1919 with his wife Dorothy, and it was probably during this later visit that he first discovered the perfect Pythagorian proportions of the Romanesque church of St. Hilaire ("Not by usura Saint Hilaire," 45/230) as well as the paradisal illumination of the Tour Maubergeon above the Hall of Justice ("the room in Poitiers where one can stand / casting no shadow," 90/619). But the Poitiers that Pound describes in 1912—a place with all the sleepy provincial charm of Germantown, Pa. or Utica, N.Y.—is not yet the mythical city of the *Cantos*. The real Poictiers (as his archaic spelling makes clear) still lies elsewhere—a locus as elusive as *trobar clus*.

After a day of sightseeing, Pound caught a night train to Angoulême—a city whose "niggly" 19th-century ecclesiastical architecture by Abadie seemed to him a prime example of the decline of French culture from the radiant ratios of St. Hilaire into the "ornament of bigotry, superstition, and mess" (LE, 151).

POITIERS

There are here many rose bushes pleached against many walls. And Notre-Dame-La-Grande has a face older than anything I know or care about though it was in fact built under Count Guillaume's eyes—with scant assistance from him.[1]

Here am I, then, in the mother city, laying about me with irrational and emotional discriminations, violating all Hueffer's canons and principles of prose, not so much through volition as through impuissance to do otherwise.[2] I say well the mother city for it was Aquitaine or if you like Limoges which raised up song again, and it was this Count Guillaume who set the fashion for the district, and if Henry began the cathedral here his grandfather & his son began & continued the trobar and at the court of the Plantagenet princes sang Daniel & De Born and Borneil and as I continue you will find many another

3

Poitiers. St Radegonde.

Poitiers. Notre-Dame-la-Grande.

4

troubadour of whom it is written, *"Si fos de Limousi."*[3] He was of Limousin, a courteous man, or a man of little generation, or something else of that sort.

And anyone who objects to the manner & form of their singing, to canzoni or cansos is as foolish as a man would be if he objected to growing roses on a trellis. And no one could sit here at this window and believe that there is any folly in growing roses in that manner.

Being modern one must have more matter and long introductory similes are demoded otherwise one might do more than record the one canzoni that was not written.

> Si com li flors
> > qui entrecima
> E florise, oloroz
> E no pren dans, ni engain
> De bois pets croizats[4]

As the rose taketh no harm from trellis, so is my love unharmed by the strait bonds she puts upon me—and so on.

As the the rose lurketh in trellis so do my thoughts in the words I must speak straitly to protect my lady from gossip
> > and so on to the envoy.

Songs, as the rose in trellis hath no harm of slight bars of crossed wood so shall the sense of your words take no harm from the rimes, for I have nailed and crossed them cunningly. Increase them before my lady who hath so crossed me that I may now be uncrossed, as I hear the touch of her thorns.

> I have seen my lady on
> her little balcony, afeeding
> the minnows in the Clain
> with bread crumbs, so that she
> seemed kindly & considerate
> but me she feedeth with
> far slighter sustenance.
> > etcetera

It is a town built like the board of pigs-in-clover,[5] terraced not without design so that each room of house and each street that skirts the slope would offer new obstacle and new exposure to the ridge against the town. I say this hard upon my canzon because you know how little I want to see the place as it is. Diane and statues of Minerva do not concern me. I have for impious reason left the tapers on the shrine of St. Radegonde and I pray that they cure me of metaphors.[6]

The worst side comes first upon you—out of a plain of poplars and flat rivers—a scurry of houses burrowing into cliff, and thus modernity, such forces as damned the soul of Mansard hurl themselves upon one.[7] I was discouraged. The people wore the clothing of Milan and Paris, the cathedral is too newly whitewashed, the faint hopes aroused by the portal of St. Porchaire faded again, and I came upon a quiet street, empty of people. Poictiers, said I, has the charm of Germantown or Utica. There are here quiet gardens but this is not what I came for. All of which evils befell me for my natural sin, to wit, that of having come into Poictiers obviously & by steam contrivance.

For Poictiers is trobar clus[8] and as uninteresting as the poetry of which you complain. Poictiers is elusive.

Along the rue des Carolus over the bridge of the Clain, in five minutes you have lost the city. For this cause the city is old, old as the galleries in the cliff below the profaning gilt of our lady's statue.[9] This is a place of exploit and defiance, a town of fourteen exits. One knowing the lie of things might lead in and out ten cavalcades under the eye of an [illegible]. To the detail it is the same, the narrow door backed for preference by a turn of stairs, [. . .] irrefutable way, a descent of street, then steps behind a square of wall, go down into a little pareis[10] before the open doors, and one sees in and to the apse which is stone. The daubed garish colour of medieval skillsless decorator who managed so well to use bungled detail for a true effect. For the shape of the towers and the court yard to the left of entrance, even the books of reference do not attempt to shake my "flair." And if the old women selling candles outside the paroisse have been renewed they do not show it.

All of these things so far as I know them stand in an air cool and exquisite & impersonal, it is the "clar temps,"[11] with nothing of the "warm south" in it.

ANGOULÊME

The medieval sin of "luxuria" approaches one by subtle gradation. Thus to be slung from a crag in a strange place about which one knows nothing & where there is nothing that one is bound to see & admire, is to let this shadowy old villain seem to offer an easy approach allowing one at the least a sense of comfort.

In the dark which the lightning did little to diminish, I seemed slung in a basket over the suburb Houmeau, or at least in some turret stuck outward from a tower's face.[12]

An hour before dawn the Charente caught enough light to break the mist and the houses of the suburb lay in grey like those in the 17th century maps of London.

With the day all this is closer, the descent less sheer, and the plain stretching northward without great interest.

The episcopal watch tower, for want of a better guess, this Angoulême, at least no troubadour whom I can recall has mentioned it.

When I implied there was nothing to see here I tampered with verity. There is a cathedral for connoisseurs,[13] my real objection is to the idea that one come to "see" or that all travel is to study the phases of architecture visigothic or otherwise, or that one should tap a certain cask of emotions in the teeth of every cathedral.

If one wish sensation from Architecture one had better stay in New York, provided that is one can separate sheer delight in mass & line from sentiment & lust for age.[14]

It may be objected that I contradict myself, that I make & write of a sheer voyage of sentiment, that I say I come to feel rather than to see.

Permit me my distinctions, and that sentiment is the father of lies (G),[15] that I am interested in, that I am a lover of strange & exquisite emotions, that I find this last in no way incompatible with the "scientific spirit." I say "scientific spirit" because the term "realism" is jaded and loaded with too many connotations.

Spinoza has left us a general catalogue of the emotions[16] but I want something different, something if you will more irregular. I would rather know the precise nature of a thing than find an apt or even an irrefutable definition.

Let me accept the designation realist, if one do not mean by it the generation Balzac-Zola-Bennet, their method if you like, but with this secession. Not everything is interesting or rather not everything is interesting enough to be written into novels, which are at all but the best a dilution of life.[17] It is excellent doubtless for future sociologists that certain diagnoses of certain strata be recorded, but it is work for encyclopedists or else it isn't, let me return to myself.

The use of dogma, generalities, inexact "ideas" had led to such a general ignorance that the impressionistic or realistic method was the only escape from it. But now we are come upon the obverse, a tendency to germanize which is philology or novels or what you will,—a failure in synthesis, a failure to recognise what is a type, a failure to see where description of a thing is worth while either because it is normal or because extreme.

Chalais and Ribérac

Leaving Angoulême behind, Pound struck out on foot in the direction of Chalais, some fifty kilometers to the south. His route took him through the small villages of La Couronne, Claix, Blanzac, and Montmoreau; following along the river Tude, he arrived at Chalais two days later. Pound's notebook jottings sketch his initial impressionistic sensations of the terrain—a gentle rolling landscape stippled with poplars and cedars out of Hobbema and Corot that seemed to him a gateway to a *"terre sainte"* or promised land.

Upon arriving in Chalais, Pound inspected its castle, perched on a small bluff overlooking the poplar-lined river Tude. He was eager to get a firsthand look at the site on account of the reference to the "vicountess of Chales" in Bertrand de Born's *"Dompna pois de me no'us chal"*—a poem whose "composite lady," Pound speculated, concealed the hidden topography of Bertran's military designs on a strategic network of castles that he sought to ally against his enemy, the count of Périgord:

> And all his net-like thought of new alliance?
> Chalais is high, a-level with the poplars.
> Its lowest stones just meet the valley tips
> Where the low Dronne [*sic*] is filled with water-lilies.
> ("Near Perigord")

Donated to the township in 1883 by the Prince de Talleyrand Périgord, the castle had been transformed into a hospice for the elderly, a fitting emblem for the decrepitude of the modern era as against the vanished glamor of troubadour times:

> At Chalais
>   is a pleached arbour;
> Old pensioners and old protected women
> Have the right there—
>   it is charity.
> I have crept over old rafters,
>   peering down
> Over the Dronne [*sic*],
>   over a stream full of lilies.
> ("Provincia Deserta")

8

The round tower & the church of Blanzac, hiding behind its hill, with some curious structure of older bld. to support the tower.

an abbey hid in cedars

CHALAIS

"May was the month & soft
"The singing nights .... "

M. H.[2]

May is the month and I have done my dix sept kilometres from Mont-moreau mostly in the devil's own down-pour. My clothing dries in the kitchen and I make my compliments to the country, especially the reach midway between Mt Moreau & Montboyer for the divergency of its slopes, for variety in the nature and disposition of its trees, for the diversity of grey which the rain there—and presumably elsewhere—is in its veil capable of assuming.

In this Chalais lived the vicountess of Bertran's Dompna Soiseubuda, of whom he found

Chalais. Château de Talleyrand-Périgord.

From Chalais, Pound walked eastward toward Aubeterre where, judging fror remembrances of this *locus amoenus* in The Pisan Cantos, he stopped by riverside inn (the Hotel de Périgord?) at the outskirts of town:

> the inn low by the river's edge,
> the poplars; to set here the roads of France
> Aubeterre, the quarried stone beyond Poitiers—
> (76/469)

> and at Aubeterrre
> or where they set tables down by small rivers,
> and the stream's edge is lost in grass
> (80/523)

Following the river Dronne, he then passed through Bourg-du-Bost on his w Ribérac, birthplace of Arnaut Daniel. Pound's observations of the vernal lands around Ribérac show him casting around for an idiom more responsive to the *ge loci* of Provençal song than the purely philologic scenery conveyed by the archaism his early translations of *il miglior fabbro*.

CLAIX AND BLANZAC

The square of St. Peter campanile follows thru the overcrowded rd. to L Couronne.[1]
Here is the round tower of chateau sheltered & flanked with poplars, hospita- ble by its avenue of approach & the long oblong stone & lurking within from one of them, now that the hay is cut, there is still the tower, behind a pale green foreground.

a little style—formal entrance to nowhere, unless it is a park that shows the wet reach of land southward & all Angoulême in retrospect.

some stones to which one listens

ruins of monstrous abbey in the dip beyond

From the hill above Claix one goes ones head above water,
        Angoulême without beauty of detail

The next moment descent above Campagne—bent trees toward a Corot, tufted poplars after Hobbema & in the elbow of the road the 1st black cedars of the terre sainte.

"De chales [la] vescomtal
la gola els manz amdos"[3]

This town is therefore worthy of remembrance not so much for its fidelity to a perhaps mistaken cause as for one throat incomparable & two handy dedications made.[4]

If this lady or De Born knew such a pleached alley as that of the castle above me, they may well have been recompensed for the infernal bother of living in the middle ages. Yet for all its drawbridges still slung, for all its archer's loop holes one can not be sure whether or no it was this castle or the one some few miles southward. Roche Chalais. For the purpose of literary effort there is nothing to choose from here. The gulf of mist is beautiful & Roche is still country imagined. Roche Chalais is on the authority of gossip downstairs a new affair and I take oath on at least one winding stairs in this mass on the hill here, to say nothing of a labyrinth inexplicable or tiny rooms in one of the turrets, a later affair than the stairs, but of a mediaeval humour.

AUBETERRE

It is on the hill rd. to Aubeterre that the fortress Chalais first shows the strength & the variety, from the height one feels the caged battlements.

After yesterday's rain she is set squarely into the heavy clouds, and the tips of the tallest poplars come just flush with the base of the wall, for all the reparations of the XVIII century, the strength of the position still communicates itself by the sense of crouch & spring in the masonry.

To the north a round watch tower beckons, & one leaves it regretfully convinced that it is really the [illegible] & the older pile.

The route to Aubeterre may be properly termed walking. The rd. takes the height suddenly with patches of wheat green, tawn grey & yellow-green, you look about you, with what purples & purple-greys beside you.

There is a certain sociability of clouds when the horizon seems lower than we are. Thus to a ruined villa with a church-like barn.

Aubeterre.

A tree with what after to be pink wisteria blossoms & a defensible wall hung with flowers.

A steep gulley carries us into the concave side of Aubeterre, disclosing the plaisance of a late chateau, the square tower of a drawbridge of sorts & the arena of green laid eastward.

To the other side is presiding the sheer wall of the castle with one crumbling bay.

The ideal village scene which Ribeyrac denies us.
In no razo have I found name of Albaterre.[5]

The Dronne full of water lilies runs to castle

RIBÉRAC

As for Ribeyrac: thru' a flat land one goes there—until Aubeterre stands like a
white tomb stone flat between two mounds—thru' a land of willows & of
poplars set in squares about low floodable fields.

A. D.
ref.   –new grain
springs in the current[6]

Before Aubeterre I find also the proper garden, the close, *vergier*, of the
poems, the antithesis of *cambra*, yes.[7]
Also I have seen magpies & blood red lilies & a cart such as Venus has in the
Roman de la Rose, and this garden was no garden in particular, just a secret
sort of walled, & hidden by a double barrier of trees, & having one great
bunch of yellow roses to give it heart & savor.
Still the lilies are not philological, and as someone might confuse *vergier* & *ort*,
and [illegible] *prada*[8]
I make this note of it

The rose of the hedge both
white & red
have given me heart to
pluck up song again
as the thin petals
of the wild hedge rose
are the 5 thoughts that
my mind has of her[9]

One goes up into mixed wood toward Bourg du Bost, with a black head of
pines in the far before one, & then into wilder growth.
In the Bourg I found an old man who knew of Daniel de Ribeyrac,
Guillaume de la Tour, & *lui de Mareuil*.[10]
Bertrand de Born, not Pons [de] Chapdueil. —Chapdueil he said held from

the lord La Tour Blanche & there was nothing there.[11] Aubeterre belonged to "Bertrand" if I remember rightly, & he knew of no other troubadours.

As for Ribeyrac, now that I am here, it is a fine place for a villa & no place at all for a castle. It has height & view & a low valley running thru' it, but neither does it bar the valley nor would it be defensible from the head of its slope even if Daniel had owned the castle which he presumably did not he might have done far worse than leaving it.[12] Besides the town shows no trace of having been fortified, it is not built for defense & there is no ruin. There is however at *Celles* the Tour de la Rigale.

Mareuil and Périgueux

After following the Dronne to Ribérac, Pound turned northward toward Mareuil, birthplace of the troubadour dubbed "the lesser Arnaut" by Petrarch. The central figure in Pound's Browningesque monologue "Marvoil" (1909), Arnaut de Mareuil's "simplicity of adequate speech" ranked him "among the best of the courtly 'makers'" (SOR, 57).

The route north covered some forty kilometers, its uphill switchbacks reminding Pound of the rhythms of the sestinas that Arnaut Daniel was credited with inventing in this region. After inspecting the dilapidated castle of Mareuil, Pound looped back down toward the southeast for another fifty kilometers, making his way through Brantôme and on into Périgueux, plagued by rain the whole way. Despite the inclement weather, the relatively wild landscape of this part of the Périgord Blanc obviously appealed to him, for in mid-August 1919, he again returned to the area for a brief walking tour with T. S. Eliot.

A week into his walking tour, Pound arrived in Périgueux (or "Perigord," as he often called it in his poetry, following what he took to be Provençal usage) to discover a city whose soaring architecture uncannily reminded him of New York. The carnival atmosphere of the annual Feast of the Trinity—torch lights and dancing on the square of the Byzantine cathedral of St. Front—caught the bedraggled traveler up in its euphoria. "Provincia Deserta" recalls this leg of the journey:

I know the roads in that place:
Mareuil to the north-east,
        La Tour,
There are three keeps near Mareuil,
And an old woman,
        glad to hear Arnaut,
Glad to lend one dry clothing.

I have walked
        into Perigord,
I have seen the torch-flames, high-leaping,
Painting the front of that church;
Heard, under the dark, whirling laughter.
I have looked back over the stream
        and seen the high building.
Seen the long minarets, the white shafts.

CELLES AND LA TOUR-BLANCHE

But about 1 m. from Ribeyrac back of Villetoureix one has a mound of the proper shape, the declivity where a wall might have fallen, surmounted by a tower the size & shape of a silo.

Villetoureix itself is not unpromising & a little beyond there is an old tower built into a house.

The rd. to Celles is indeed a sort of sestina, of cusp & hills, of prospects opened & shut, or round trees & poplars aligned.

sestina vs. recurrence in nature

Above Celles the road is steep & long ending in a pine ridge whence one should see perhaps Aubeterre over toward Angoulême to the N.E. & Perigueux, but the land on all sides is thick with rain. I parted with St. Martial to the E. & Chapdeuil at Bourg des Maisons about a mile to the west & the rain displayed a persistence that I felt I should [illegible].[1]

I sheltered myself in some stone quarries & won thru the next of it to la Tour on a high plain of the style favoured by the first illustrators of Byron.

& the white Tour is a fine square ruin on a fine square pedestal but the charm of the village is the ruined chateau, the restaurant "tenu par Dessiris,"—Rembrandt Interior—Fr. t. 1670,

Marquis de Cabaud

Well walled house at ? Cercles

MAREUIL

The road is uphill again to Mareuil & there are upon it towers square, gabled & homely, at la chapelle Montabourlet.

2 moats
1 inside wall ›
drawbridge

At vieux Mareuil we have a church with thick walls, with battlements at the corners & what may have been the upper slant of a portcullis. The walls are higher than the domes which are well built but have much loose stone lying about them. This fortification seems to me in all likelihood the remains of the castle where Arnaut saw daylight. The transept was made very early XIII. The tower is new. The present mill stream may well have provided a moat.

La Tour Blanche looks like a church transformed. I shall not number the other towers upon the route on the way one ascends thru a pine wood & turns down the winding valley to Brantôme.

On the right of my way was a low ruin of two towers, and finding no approach I drowned my self in the long grass to reach it.

      Roses & violets what dogs here hiding. —

Oh well, whose arms so ever you like, here are more broken turrets and winding fallen stairs overrun with garden and dogs to bay you to death. The violets are I admit an anachronism and this is not *the* chateau of Mareuil, but there are roses enough to make up for it.

Mareuil lies on the other road from Ribeyrac, and from the town approach seems mostly chimneys.

Here if ever should one go back.

This route for one that is not chemin d'état has a curious direction over the highest hill the castle going with him but about a mile of it. From which crest

Mareuil-sur-Belle. Le Vieux Château.

the present building shows it proudest, a thing, to pardon the rhetoric, with the centuries written out upon it; the round towers, drawbridges, the high slate gables of the XIIIe.

Make what vaunt they can of seigneural tenure, & even in the mutilated church we find

"Sigismonde Charlotte
Laure de Hautefort b. 1799—d. 1847
barring the tablet "au troubadour Arnaut de Mareuil," for here have we the finest of castles in the vilest déshabillé. A court yard in mediaeval filth a chapel full of straw and implements. It was sacked last year & given over to insult?

The fashion of it is this, that moat is within the walls, or rather there are in a fashion 2 moats one surrounding the whole castle, and it has in it rabbits instead of water and the standing towers which you may mount over broken stairs if you hold it worth the risk must be of later date. Yet they give one so clear a hint of life at least 500 years forgotten that I may as well describe the pattern of them as well as I may. In one tower, there seemed to be uniformly floor by floor, a large square room with one deeply recessed window, a room of convenience, and a little cupboard like a servant's room in the wall.

The oubliettes were dark & I had no means of seeing them.

The chapel was in the wall over the moat & the watchman's comfortable nitch commanded both this and the moat bridge by opposite slits.

All this should be more recent than the time of the not particularly fortunate poet whose name adorns the outer wall.

The whole castle is set flat in the fields. The wall is in different sort of masonry.

According to all information available the family of Talleyrand Perigord owned not only this but all the other castles of Dordogne.[2]

BRANTÔME AND AGONAC

Toward Agonac
Puychantu 6–2. K.

Here, having learned all that I thought it possible for me to learn from the

11 degrees & differences of the sensational, I bought an umbrella to which the gentle reader owes the ensuing pages. Thus by the timely expenditure of 2.50 fr. were these inestimable memoirs continued to the pleasure & instruction not only of my own generation but of many who shall come after me.

At Lespres there is a house with a great beautiful garden. It was built for the Bishops mistress & has a carefully cut nitch on one corner.

Chateau l'Eveque supports its fortified dignity but a slight way beyond.

PÉRIGUEUX

To write in praise of a city wherein one arrives after 50 miles on unaccustomed feet may remain for him "to whom grace reserveth experience." Périgueux is approached through a solid mile of slum ill paved & ill attended, in this I found no alleviation except one girl with a solferino bow in her hair and a rather more than middle sized dog with an intelligent expression.

To write in praise of food when one has broken the day's full fast on nothing more than coffees & a pocket full of brioches would be indiscreet & undiscriminating.

Yet this tower at Brantôme & St Front of Périgueux may well have been seen by many another in like pain. The tower by many a jongleur if the

Périgueux. Cathedral of St Front.

benedictine abbey harboured such, & by most them. St Front of Périgueux!
St. Front.[3] What a cathedral—& San Christo what an approach what fine im-
moral music, a street flowing with pennons, [to] the left a showman's drums,
to the right the whirl for dance, what mediaeval windings & turnings, & in
the space before sanctuary some sort of a fête in progress with a merry-go-
round, no modern contraption but one as one reads of in "Pèlerinage Charlemagne,"[4] a thing of tinsel, of crystal, of crystal in ruby & white, a thing of
thrones, & howdahs, & lit by a flare of gasoline like a torch flare, and behind
it, what a cathedral! Be on your guard San Marco, here are domes against
your domes, & a tower along your tower, & who in the darkness shall
remember the gold that lines you or its glamour in your fort?[5]

Here also is laughter & light, & music, and a rattle of accoutrements & here
are domes of Byzant, & pattern of the east.

Pass there, & the stream of L'Isle throws up to us a scant dozen of reflected
lamps & above us the inexplicable line cuts the darkening lavender. Return
and the faces in the crowd are gay,[6] and simple, are primitive, approach
deliria, and are for strangers suspicious, tending to be afraid, and by the drum
a fellow dances in a smock to his knees.

Tis the feast of the Trinity, here, at least, little is changed.[7]

Hautefort.

Château de Hautefort.

Hautefort

Stronghold of the counts of Périgord, the city of Périgueux was closely associated in Pound's mind with Bertran de Born—and particularly with the strategic network of castles mentioned in his *"Dompna pois de me no'us cal."* Convinced that only a firsthand inspection of the lay of the land could solve the riddles of the poem, Pound set out to explore the terrain to the east of Périgueux—the preparatory topographical fieldwork for his 1915 poem "Near Perigord."[1]

Pound's first stop was Hautefort—the castle in the title of his 1909 "Sestina: Altaforte" and citadel of the "spit-cat" Bertrand de Born:

> And our En Bertrans was in Altafort,
> Hub of the wheel . . .
> . . . on that great mountain of a palm—
> Not a neat ledge, not Foix between its streams,
> But one huge back half-covered up with pine
> > ("Near Perigord")

Pursuing his research into the landscape of Bertran's poetry, Pound also hiked through the wooded terrain around the tiny hilltop hamlet of Blis-et-Born, situated above the Auzévère river to the east of Périgueux. His notes show him still trying to decipher the reticulated topographical "web" of strongholds that he believed Born had attempted to "spread like the fingertips of one frail hand" against his enemy, "Tairiran," count of Périgord.

Although only mentioned in passing in his manuscript, Pound's encounter in Blis-et-Born with "a man at work" was apparently memorable enough to be recalled in The Pisan Cantos as an exemplary instance of peasant hospitality extended toward a lost Odysseus:

> and the red-bearded fellow was mending his
> > young daughter's shoe
> "Me Hercule!   c'est notre commune"
> ("Borr," not precisely Altaforte)
> > with such dignity
> > > (80/523)

ALTAFORT

Altafort is, as I have said, rebuilded,[2] but it is set in a great nave of a hill, to match the brag of its Born, backed with pine wood steep, breathlessly steep to south and lording it over two far stretches of valley, so that for long the fiery chatelain might have seen them burning his trees, & trampling down his grain.[3] Here, then, came they foe & friend alike whetted at the chance of getting rid once for all of this spit-cat de Borñr here drove they his beasts, slaughtered his peasants & wrought up the mood in him:

qt.

Even now the position is not such that one would move machinery against it, and a man walking even [among] such smaller towers as held here in the old days might well have grown thoughts beyond his station, seeing so much land & nothing in it to withstand him

Except, . . . except

The south rd. toward Montignac with Midonz Maent at the end of it.[4]

When I consider Altafort rebuilded
& Chalais as a hospice for old men
Apenas quel cor nom fanh
Per las baros armatz
E li pros descroizats
Al mien [illegible]
It is not Time hath [illegible]
Mas li fins jauzimens
e Donas des altres tems
Qu era ben ben laudatz
amatz y desamatz
Come notazan[5]

That is, going my way amid this ruin & beauty it is hard for me at times not to fall into the melancholy regarding that it is gone, & this is not the emotion that I care to cultivate for I think other poets have done so sufficiently.

BLIS-ET-BORN

Born itself is a prime nest for highwaymen.[6] You come at it through a bridlepath the entrance of which almost concealed. Tho it stands sheer from the cross road, a wide path skirts the stream, reaching into the hill, watching itself from clumps of underbrush, watching the high rd.—winding thru a field speckled white with daisies following the base of hills & ascending. It is over hung by a strong farm, gaunt above the poppy-field at Bliss.

   & he would be a bold man who would try it at night—in times uncertain.

—Also for strategy, it runs from main rd. to main rd. in two loops.

so that you can go out or not, as you choose.

   Staying inside this bottle with 3 necks, I found it opening out into some fairly wide half cultivated fields, where after it became so serpentine & so full of choices for walking in & in on a spiral that only after I had won up to the level of scrub pine & convinced myself that I was lost for a night at least, did I come to two farms commanding a wide view & another opportunity for descent,

   then by the grace of god I came to a man at work who directed me to an inn without a sign.[7] Hence by foot path by a final scrabble of sheer rock I came upon Born itself, which is the summit, & is the key I should think to some further complexity, for what I had expected to be "main rd." to Cubjac was evidently part of the network.

   From Born & from this rd. you have the valleys beneath you. Borr̃r̃r

Chateau de M. le Moulinard. —Bliss et Born

2.7. —apparently on a sheer needle in the midst of things it must overlook the Auvézère

? new house in foreground

another ruin on the rd. near Cubjac

which things being so & which things being ascertained, I would fain have dragged my remains to rest in the next valley, at Savignac-les-églises, at an inn there, but this inn being filled with a captain & three men @ arms I took tramway for Excideuil in that prescience which occasionally descends when after we have done our utmost the perfect thing awaits.

Perdu: Petite chienne jaune / répond au nom de *Lôve*.[8]

Excideuil

Only fifteen kilometers from Hautefort on the river Loue, Excideuil was the birthplace of Giraut de Borneil (or Bornelh), the *"maestre del trobadors"* praised by Dante in *De Vulgari Eloquentia*, as the model poet of moral rectitude (SOR, 48–53). But Pound's 1912 observations of the place (here reproduced in their original notebook lineation) focus primarily on the architectural features of its castle—which was besieged on three occasions by Richard Coeur de Lion in 1182 during the uprising against the Plantagenets that had presumably been fomented by Bertran de Born, "stirrer-up of strife."

Pound returned to Excideuil in mid-August 1919, where he and his wife Dorothy were joined by Eliot. The visit is memorialized in Canto 29, with Eliot's name honorifically transformed into Arnaut:

> So Arnaut turned there
> Above him the wave pattern cut in the stone
> Spire-top alevel the well-curb
> And the tower with cut stone above that, saying:
>> "I am afraid of the life after death."
> and after a pause:
> "Now, at last, I have shocked him."
>
> (29/145)

The visual mapping of the scene is characteristically precise: looking westward from the castle bluff, the well-curb in its courtyard (which Pound had apparently repaired for the old woman who lived in the run-down manor) would indeed be alevel the spire of the church of St. Thomas in the town of Excideuil below.[1] The "wave pattern" in the stonework of the parapets would later come to serve as Excideuil's hieratic signature of place in the paradisal geography of The Pisan Cantos, where the castle is rhymed with two other cosmic fortresses, Ecbatana ("the city of Dioce whose terraces are the colors of stars") and Montségur—water, air, and fire:

> Nancy were art thou?
> Whither go all the vair and the cisclatons
> and the wave pattern runs in the stone
> on the high parapet (Excideuil)
> Mt. Segur and the city of Dioce
> Que tous les mois avons nouvelle lune
>
> (80/524)[2]

Excideuil. Ruins of the old château.

Excideuil. Château de
Talleyrand-Périgord.

EXCIDEUIL

A couple of great fields
set up along with the church
spire, the sky pale blue
& white after the sunset,
with the tree on the skyline
outlined against it,
& the great gentle tower

clear edged,
unascendable, and
for no known reason
these things wrought
out a sort of perfect mood
in things,
the air was after rain
damp & coolish.
The wheat in some parts
shoulder high or over it.
—The sheer drop at the
edge of the level.
& the "new" part,
the hay barn with
carved *wood* doors,
the place with the parapets,
this also, mi lady
pleasing when the
other towers were out
of fashion,

this with a thin
    chain of stars above
it, & in the side
of the delicate
round turret
the thoughtful variety
of little windows,
square, round &
oval,[3]

---

married to a minister secretary of state, peer of France & god knows what all[4]

But all these things are out of my chapters, they are of France not Aquitaine, & all these later orders mean monopoly

Chalus

The final portion of Pound's initial fortnight tour took him (mostly by rail) through the heart of the Limousin. He walked the twenty-five-kilometer stretch from St. Yrieix to Chalus (where Richard Coeur de Lion was slain in battle in 1199), before proceeding on to Rochechouart and Limoges. "Provincia Deserta" again:

> At Rochecoart [sic],
> Where the hills part
> > in three ways,
> And three valleys, full of winding roads,
> Fork out to south and north,
> There is a place of trees . . . grey with lichen.
> I have walked there
> > thinking of old days.

ST. YRIEIX

The next day wishing to reach lodging by night-fall I came by tramway to St. Yrieix. This tram carried, for the most part, wood to factory where it is changed into tanner's essence. Awaiting the tram I fell in with a comfortable man from Sarlat & he dealt likewise in garments for the dead, from him I gathered the remaining history of Haute-fort: that he remembered visiting it 20 yrs. ago when it belonged to De Damas precepteur to the king who might have been Henry V.[1] At this time there stood always a guardsman in jack boots on either side of the draw bridge & seignurial state pertained. The chateau was later sold at a bargain to Armides who'd made his fortune in the Panama scandal.

   At the hotel of Poujol[2] I came also upon this adv. worthy of memory:
> > sic transit gloria

CHALUS

The narrow-gage brought us up through scrub & thru a place once well forested, St. Yrieix has in it one inexplicable church, & one tower acrumble. Thence I came down the long slow valley to Chalard thru' broom for the most part withered, to Chalard with its church on the high spur southward, past the green mound Viellecour forest to Chalus.

Passing the latter rd. first a young lady of the better class with a duenna & a Beardseley smile, second a fire of dry twigs, which is in this land 'luck' & advances you one k. on yr. journey, "cela vous accourriez bocoup."[3]

The road gives on Chalus suddenly, the ruin high in the centre of the landscape like a great headless duck on circular nest.

In attacking this castle Richard Coeur de Lion got his death wound of an arrow, on the turn of the century 1199, as you may read in the Encyclopædia Brittanica, Baedeker & Le Petit Larousse.

What England gained by so selecting a king of the island for the barons to do what they liked with, Provence lost, for it is unlikely that the crusade would have made much headway with a Plantagenet in Aquitaine.

The town seems given to manufacture in the smallest way, & is in parts

Chalus. View of the château.

Chalus. The rock where Richard Coeur de Lion was mortally wounded (1199).

very squalid, esp. the castle quarter. There are certain very well kept gardens, numerous houses for rent, & never have I seen armorial bearing on doors more squalid. No one seems to know the reason why he or she is in the town, barring one very small person who was guarding one cow & one goat on the steep before the towers. She said the castle belonged to her, & I dare say it does. —There remain of it 3 towers, 2 on the hill, one in town itself. They are all very solid & make one wonder how any thing except dynamite & modern artillery could have any effect upon them, —except, that is, the vegetation that is nibbling the tallest top of them. The siege of 1199 must have attempted some portion of fortress long since broken into cottages. I say broken into cottages, for time has far less to do with demolition of good masonry than has the value of stone.

My left shin denying me further assistance, not wishing to remain longer at Chalus, I went by train to Rochechouart & Limoges, filled with moral reflections on the inconvenience of travel in a time when such assistance would have been denied one & when like mishap might have befallen oneself or ones beast.

Certain engaging people in their eagerness to deny that the race has progressed tell us that what we have gained in material comfort we have lost in spiritual riches. The number of interruptions to life, mental, moral or physical, —interruptions wholly beyond one's own control, must have been in the middle ages such that no belief save that of divine mercy for oneself & an

eternal hell for ones irritators would have been tenable or satisfactory. This
for the discomfort of the rd. and the boredom in the castles must easily have
been such as to warrant a special form of verse "Envez" [or] "envoi" to express
it.

Thus B de B.

(qt.)

It is undeniable that if one wishes to see objects instead of to realize conditions, he had better travel by rail. He will thus arrive at his divers destinations
with a full current of inspective energy, he will not know how to get ants out
of a jam pot, and he will not meet with a finished courtesy in unexpected
places.

I do not mean by this that the manners of the peasant are uniformly or
evenly exquisite, but simply that one finds next to the soil—now and again—a
perfect breeding.

Also it has been borne in upon me, how fully our values of comparison
change with a slight change of condition, —and walking the roads I have
found a deal more force in certain lines & stanzas than I had ever expected.

Ni gels, ni vens, ni plueva,[4]

Living in houses, or even decently equipped with aquascuta, the weather
means little to us, but the life of such lines of verse, if we consider them as
sung by men to whom the condition of the weather was a necessary concomitant of every action & enjoyment, is vastly increased, the prelude of weather
in nearly every canzon becomes self evident, it is the actual reflection.

Uzerche and Brive

Returning to the Limousin landscapes he had left behind three weeks earlier, Pound arrived by train in Uzerche on June 27 for the second three-week leg of his walking tour.

Although he had asked Dorothy to go to the British Museum to look up the precise location of Ventadour in Smith's *Troubadours at Home*, Pound did not explore the region to the east of Uzerche and Brive until his walking tours of the summer of 1919. The town of Ussel and the ruins of the castle of Eble III at Ventadour near Egletons are later mentioned in the *Cantos*, associated with one of Pound's favorite poets, Bernart of Ventadorn:

> Where was the wall of Eblis
> at Ventadour, there now are the bees,
> And in that court, wild grass for their pleasure
> That they carry back to the crevice
> Where loose stone hangs upon stone.
> (29/132)

These same ruins later reappear amid the mnemonic rubble of The Pisan Cantos, fragments of a landscape now believed to be irrevocably lost:

> el triste pensier si volge
> ad Ussel. A Ventadour
> va il consire, el tempo rivolge
> and at Limoges the young salesman
> bowed with such french politeness "No that is impossible."
> (. . .)
> Or at Ventadour the keys of the chateau;
> rain, Ussel
> (74/442, 450)

UZERCHE

You go into *Uzerche* thru' a tunnel, no railroad attempts this. This is from the north side, emerging you find several bridges leaping over each other without communicating. There are houses before you. It is probable that some very

32

large person threw down a pile of jack straws and that the houses were built on that foundation

"Who has a house in Uzerche"[1]

has, or is apt to have today a rickety turret of masonry that looks "interesting," a choice of odours & perhaps a view. I have with infinite tact and perserverance secured the latter (Hotel de France).

The town is built on a long crooked ridge almost isolated by the Vézère, I have come beyond the south gate, and had I come some centuries ago, it would have been by this gate alone that I could have entered. Thus came Uc Bacalairia & the disreputable Faidit.[2]

There is the princely Chalusset to the right of the road as one comes here, and if I have insulted Limoges I should at least make reparation to the hold of its Viscount.[3] But I should like for a time to talk of towns and town life & to leave off talking of castles & of high life and of troubadours even, tho they linked the two together, the court & the town.

It is harder for me to do this. We know, in one way, so much more of the glitter & array, yet the saddler up the road in his booth 4 x 10 can have changed little, and the smith can have changed little, & the sawyer has changed a good deal.

The curé a hundred ft. below me by the river has not changed his gown, nor the fisherman in mid stream so altered his tackle.

The smith & the miller were the first specialists undoubtedly.

The streets of Uzerche are narrow as those of Tangier and if this town still stinks this town was a rich & a strong one. Il porte sa bourgeoisie comme un marquisat was said later but I have no doubt that the burgers of the town of Uzerche looked into their metal mirrors & thought something much the same.

There were then more people in this restricted space. This city does nothing that it did not do in the middle ages. There are here all the permanent institutions—including Lilith at her window, with her hair done exactly as it is in Rossetti's portrait of her.[4] However I am in no position to talk as my hostel is on the wall. It is also built over a stable. I suspected as much. —Our friends of the primo cento had a perfect perception of the laws of gravity but no sense whatever of the corresponding laws of levitation.

The really beautiful way to see Uzerche is from the path by the river or from the lower walls where the witches pace in the cool of the evening.

As for the interior of the town, it is mostly one or 2 curving streets but a man should get drunk before he attempts the exploration otherwise his resulting ideas of it will be vague & indefinite. For my self I grant you anything, that the Chinese alphabet has clarity, that Persian artists knew perspective— anything!!

I had set out upon this book with numerous ideas, but the road had cured me of them. There is this difference, I think, between a townsman & a man doing something or going somewhere in the open, namely that the townsman has his head full of abstractions. The man in the open has his mind full of objects—he is, that is to say, relatively happy.

I left that brown skull Uzerche for the road again—a road green & bosky, mile up & mile down of it. No castle overhangs it.

BRIVE

I never know at what point a hill ceases to be a hill & becomes what should be called a mountain but I should say this [illegible] at Donzenac, at least in breadth, and certainly beyond there for it is one climb, draw & plunge into Brive, fives miles of it.

Brive.

They crown a king here in 584. Dagobert or someone of that sort and nothing has happened since.[5] The town like most valley towns has gone on improving itself, it is a little like Verona, a small colourless Verona, a little like an American village near an amusement park. Who has a house here has a castle in Provence might more readily be said than of Uzerche where the proverb belongs. —For the turrets here are more numerous, in better repair, & possibly not so old, but Brive is flat, more spread, and could never have seemed the cracked section of stage scenery for which Uzerche on its thin ridge, presents itself—not unlike a Toledo in two dimensions. Every tower of it in view. The turrets of Brive are only to be discovered by walking the streets of that town—most of them moderately clean & open. The abbey is much restored, but like the little church at [illegible] there is a lot of personality about the portal & the romanesque is good.

There is to the east of Brive a place with so fine & sinister a name that I was almost led there, altho I knew there was nothing for the eye, a name I had invented for a poem once but had never expected to find in the stone as Malemort.[6] I restrained myself however from this defection & took the jagged highway toward Toulouse past some cave dwellings at Lamouroux, to where the square gables of chateau Noailles stand over all the gorges; to where some red roofs amid the trees give one false hopes of hospice; to Cressensac. There is, across the valley in the green-wood forest, a castle once half restored (hotel Ventach), hence I wind down the gently shelving rd. to the needle-like spine of Chapelle Auzac where the valley grows long & blue again, & thence to Souillac, as I had come within hale of all the best Troubadours save Piere Vidal, Tolosan, during my 1st fortnight, it was not to be expected that I should find another land so thick with ghosts close after it.

The Dordogne

After stopping over in Souillac, Pound entered into the broad, limestone-rimmed valley of the Dordogne. His notes indicate that he followed the south bank of the river westward, then turned north toward Carlux and covered the rest of the westward path to Sarlat along country lanes, passing through St. Vincent-le-Paluel along the way. In his first drafts of the Cantos (the so-called Ur-Cantos published in 1917), Pound transforms this region of the Périgord Noir into a pagan Renaissance landscape alive with Ovidian eros. Only his Provençal spelling of the place hints at its troubadour past:

> Dordoigne! When I was there,
> There came a centaur, spying the land,
> And there were nymphs behind him.
> (Ur-Canto 2)

> (. . .)
> And the blue Dordoigne
> Stretches between white cliffs,
> Pale as the background of a Leonardo.

Proceeding southward from Sarlat, he visited the bastide of Domme, perched high above the river, and then followed the back roads through scrub pine to the hilltop town of Gourdon to the southeast, where he arrived just in time to witness the end of the festivities of St. John's Eve. Pound's sketchy observations of the colorful celebrations of Midsummer's Eve were later expanded in original draft of Canto 2 and elliptically resurface in final version of Canto 4. In these later rewritings of his visit to Gourdon, the medieval pageantry of the Saint John's Fair is interpreted as a survival of purificatory pagan fire-sacrifices associated with the fertility rites of the summer solstice.[1]

> Or Gourdon
> Juts into the sky
> Like a thin spire,
> Blue night's pulled down around it
> Like tent flaps, or sails close hauled. When I was there,
> *La noche de San Juan,* a score of players
> Were walking about the streets in masquerade,
> With pikes and paper helmets and the booths,
> Were scattered align, the rag ends of the fair.
> (Ur-Canto 2)

Torches melt in the glare
    set flame of the corner cook-stall,
Blue agate casing the sky (as at Gourdon that time)
    the sputter of resin,
Saffron sandal so petals the narrow foot: Hymenaeus Io!

(4/I5)

SOUILLAC

I came in view of the basin of grey rock, with the Dordogne as grey within it for the weather was overcast. An old man at a smoke house refused me greeting & then bawled after me that I could come in quicker by the field path. The railroad on stilts in the valley seemed to have far more trouble to do so.

There is here a real ruin. 2 sides of an abbey tower, just strong enough to hold a bell, and there is a church with a dozen apses, and within some good carving: Isaia looking like a Russian dancer and a column of beasts eating each other.[2]

Next day I took my way thru the valley, rock bare & grey to the right of it,

LE CIRQUE DE SOUILLAC

Vallée de la Dordogne

Souillac.

12. Lot — SOUILLAC — Route de Sarlat et la Dordogne au pays du Raysse

Phototypie Rezzot et Guion

Souillac.

& a chapel & house set like thin pasteboard at the other side & against the cloud, & there showed mountains [illegible] covered with a needle or two of rock beyond these, & when I reached the river itself there were poplars beside it.

& thence the road is a parapet with the river below it, grey rock, the sky bluish & whitish & the land with light subdued is like a background in Leonardo, so do his rivers curve, so do his rocks vary from white grey to dark.

Later the route goes down between plane trees, and grows dull for a bit until we come to the ford head where the branch runs up to Carlux & when the rd. leaves the river below here it is haunted & pleasant to walk by as was the rd. from Aubeterre & I came by a fine uncharted castle that stands like sheer Romance.

& this place is Paluel that was of the counts of Vigier, but who, by all the gods of irreverence, who is the Prince of Croy, is he a myth or a modern, is he a grand seigneur or a dandy of the boulevards, & who but a grand seigneur could own a chateau so hidden & a name so prehistoric.[3] Anyhow I take off my hat to him

"to all may honour increase"

It is on my conscience that I should go to Gourdon & Roc Amadour. 9408 people have been to Rocamadour & 9409 have written brilliant descriptions of it, there is at Rocamadour the black image of the virgin carved by Zacchaeus the publican who for obvious reasons traveled thither under the alias of Amadour, which is nothing less than Amator.[4] If I go to Rocamadour I shall begin a digression on religion, which would be outside the scope & purpose of this work wherein it is my intention to treat of almost everything else.

SARLAT

The city Sarlat boasts 3 troubadours of no importance, for one was C. the copyist & one was a jongleur (Aimeric de S.) & the 3d. was Giraut de Salignac.[5]

A rich city they inscribed it, & one may well believe that it was so. It is still a sumptuous ruin. The roofs are of good stone & the pavements are beneath contempt.

The inhabitants seem addicted to some peculiar disease of the eyes. It is a prime place to start the plague in & here 1st I saw men playing real 9 pins.

The denizens of large towns are, possibly, detestable, but they who dwell in small towns are immeasurably worse.

At Sarlat which is not really 1/2 so bad as I have made out, I had reached my proper land again.

There is a broad green chain of it weaving across the scale map, & this green means for the most part wooded valleys. The towns lie closer here, & by this system the troubadours went & came, when I had left this as at St. Yrieix & Brive I had found bald upland without natural magic, I had found scenery sometimes but little landscape.

At any rate, the magic seems to be natural magic, requires great trees, & a readiness for rain.

DOMME

Domme is acrest the highest cliff about here. The Dordogne winds thru the flat land below, & striking now this side of its barrier & now the other, a band of bluish metal with rippled chevrons in the shallows.

If I have made invidious remarks about scenery, I retract them, here at least one has it and landscape together.

The road leads up, along, & about the grey face of rock here. There are two gates and triple terraces of walls mostly ruined & the town within is simple.

Tho' its name arouses question on a much vexed & utterly unsettlable question of "the text."

Cill de Doma[6]

here is a Doma, much readier to hand than Pui de Dome by Clermont.

Doma in the sight line, Montignac, Sarlat, Gourdon & not out of memory of Périgueux.

But à bas la Philologie etc. below me the oxen are diminished in stature, the new mown fields seem as close of weave as does an ingrain carpet.

From Domme a path leads right over the wild top of things. I lost myself in fields then found the rd. & went down thru miles of pine wood, & little good it did me, for I was far off my way before I met the post man. By the tree at the + rds in the field take the left track with the ruts. The least promising. From a few ft. along it you can see Gourdon clear on its hill in the distance.

GOURDON

& all rds have an ending so I came finally down out of the pine wood, down even to poplars & mown grass & climbed at last into Gourdon. This place sits on its peak alertly. Spectat et spectatur.[7] The far hills were already dark blue with a little grey in it & the sun blinked from the wet poplar leaves as from a 1000 bits of mirrour.

As I came in by the street of Cavaignac past the restaurant Fourgons I feel sure the last Pict is not dead here.

The logia beside the church portal makes the central square not unlike that of an Italian village, & the keep of Wm. 9 was I suppose the natural tower of rock level with the church roof & walled still, in various degrees, the church has battlements ? just above the door.

& somehow it was rather fun to walk about this place in the blue of the evening, for the blue, clear, a little lavender, was drawn close to one, & close in at the sides, for the peak of Gourdon is so narrow that all streets ended in it, & no street was long. The sky was for once like a tent really, & not the plainsman's basin.

Also it is "la noche de San Juan," and various players are about with pikes & halbards & the stage is & as should be all stages proper, 4 planks & 4 crossbeams, out of Rojas, or out of Lope.[8] —At any rate four days of heavy walking have brought me once more over the border. I knew it was feasible.

Albi and Toulouse

Once again "over the border" into the real southland, his imagination filled with the "plains of romance," Pound traveled by train through the rugged mountains and valleys of Le Quercy, stopping at Cahors and Rodez along the way. From Rodez, he walked southwest to Albi via Naucelle and Carmaux, and then followed the river Tarn to Gaillac and Rabastens, before hopping a train at Montastruc that took him on into Toulouse. All in all, he covered some 150 kilometers on foot in the space of four days.

The most important 12th-century center of Provençal poetry under the enlightened reign of the counts Raimon, Toulouse attracted such major troubadours as Peire Vidal, Bernart de Ventadour, Aimeric de Peguilhan, and Folquet de Marseilles. A century later, passing through the city on a pilgrimage to Spain, Guido Cavalcanti here met his muse Mandetta in the church of La Daurade on the banks of the Garonne—the river that was to have provided the title for the projected published version of Pound's 1912 walking tour. The various allusions to Toulouse (or "Tolosa") in the *Cantos*, however, all seem to refer to his subsequent stay in the city in the spring and summer of 1919—over the course of which he wrote a series of essays on French history and literature published in *The New Age* as "Pastiche: The Regional."

CAHORS AND RODEZ

Cahors & Rodez: not that one should see, or sees them, for some names are so heavy with unreality that we can never find them—not tho' our senses deceive us.

Troy, with a horse outside it, is possibly to be discovered, but these planes are of romance itself, I may have been to them, for surely one remembers Le Sieur de Rodez with his hand sticking out of the midmost of four castles built about each other & about, & Cahors is in Dante with the mystical beasts, but that one walk into these places & out of them, ah no.[1] This is to be doubted.

Cahors has a river about it. In all likelihood this river girdles the city seven times & then ascends in a waterspout & looses itself in Lethe, or something of that sort. And Rodez is a Greek island, probably,—at least there was one.

I admit that I have been in places having names like these, but no one fed me pomegranates, & I doubt if I could return.

I have some memory of a place to the south of Gourdon of cloisters cut in

41

lime, of a bridge machicolated, in this place the air is good & the beer is passable, & there is no reason whatever why anyone should go there & the valley of the Lot is I should say wilder than that of the Dordogne & the land is on edge between there & Rodez—a city of no mean enchantment.

No, but a great thing set on a mountain with a great cathedral in the midst of it, reddish, full of rose windows, & meagre of door ways.

ALBI

From *Rodez*, 3 days walking brought me to Albi, on the high plateau of Segala (Cigala) thru the cold wet air. Crossed Aveyron, below Rodez, small & narrow as a creek, & the Viaur by a great bridge at Tanus. And either of these streams would bring you to St. Antonia, and a little below it to Penne, which was Pena d'Albegis, & then to Montalban which was they say Montaldon, or Montaudon of the priory.[2]

The Viaur scarcely wider where it flows under the long viaduct between dark brown rocks at Tanus, by the steep of the Ramfort tower.

The weather was gay & warm as I set out from Naucelle with a tag of Vidal's rattling about my thorax—

E tot quant es d'avinan[3]

& no one to object when I sang off the key.

Peire d'Alverne
has a throat
sings like a frog in the moat,[4]

Well, the type repeats itself & it was such a day as makes a walking tour worth while, there was the smell of hay in the air, & everything was blue & green so I finished off the distance to Albi, as there seemed nothing better to do.

I have seen also a lizard, a peacock, & some gypsies who were driving down the same route after the fair of St. John in Rodez, & who seemed well pleased that I could keep up with them.

& I have seen the town of Carmaux which is nothing much to see—a brickish blotch full of smoke stacks.

Above Carmaux the earth turns sandy, & this aided perhaps by the declining light made it seem as if one were approaching the sea. Then the plain showed a number of great dunes with no city upon any of them, & then to the right of the rd. appeared the tower Notre Dame which, the dazzle of the sun behind it, might have been either church or castle.

Then the great brick side of Albi cathedral to a hill in front of me.

Further there shone a tower to the left of the way & this might be, but probably is not, the "old castle" of Aimar lo Ners.[5]

As for Albi it is old, inhospitable,—no good cafes meet one at entrance, & the cathedral is fortified down to the river—the Tarn—an inkish green, and the crusade might have been a decade ago for nothing is repaired here (except for the cathedral which is being TOO much repaired) but the place seems falling to pieces & half deserted, and houses are built down to the water, over all sorts of arches.

The cathedral is a new affair in any case. 1277 they began it—when the gai savoir was dead, it is so with a number of antiquities here & here abouts, even the very swagger of the bulwarks of Aigues Mortes will be no use to me.[6]

It can not be denied that this cathedral is an oddity, for it looks like a great oblong keep & is of new brick mostly.

Within it one finds some interesting carving & a little good glass.

Which things being ascertained I went out again into that curious light which I noticed yesterday & which has a suggestion of the sea in it.

I went down a dull flat road with the chalky cliffs on my right hand & found one of them, a ruined chateau, lifted a tower as narrow as a giant chimney stack, & as little adorning as Lipton in London or a great narrow pill bottle.

In a field I saw a woman cutting her good-man's hair, & doing it badly.

At Gaillac one came to real Midi—a blaze of Italian sun on the semi-spanish houses. Here the wise man stays in his café, & the fool is peripatetic.

When the heat of the day was broken, I went on, with a light low rainbow to the left, & stopped that night at L'Isle d'Albi, or L'Isle sur Tarn for the name amused me. (Blaye near Carmaux)

This town is jumble of bricks & crossbeams and out-jutting second stories, & the church is a quaint bit of brick work, haunted & dark, & with a pale stage lighting that brings its statues unpleasantly near to life.

The town square is formed by a colonnade, like those in the Italian towns.

It is true that the inky Tarn and all this country were once dyed with blood, but it is late to cry over the spilling.[7] Dante put that swine F.D.M. (Folquetus de Marsilia) in paradise on most unsatisfactory credentials.[8]

RABESTANS

The next day I came into Rabastens under a pale sky, & into Montastruc, & then to avoid the slums I took train into Toulouse.

It is the city of Vidal & the counts Raimon & of Bull Fights & Clemence Isaure & about all that remains of the city as Vidal knew it is the church St.—.

Rabastens. Church
interior, Notre-
Dame-du-Bourg.

Toulouse. The
handwriting on the
face of the postcard
is Ezra Pound's.

Toulouse.

Toulouse.
Saint-Sernin.

44

Rabastens a really interesting church. Fresco later, but style-effect medieval.[9]

Red, & such a red, beautiful brick, lustre of copper. Ladies in trailing white, Tristan & Ysolt bar the halos, before a monk. Angels with geometric wings,—arms & blazons—like walking into a mss—blue like Sorrento but darker, greenish blue & knights in crusading armour & an orange background in same register, this for an angel, & bars & swastikas & glass—probably modern but wonderfully chosen, a gallery above apse with figures between arches, & the ceiling full of painted holes with people looking thru'.

Parts, but never an ensemble like this. The nave might have been the grt hall in court of Count of Limoges.

One of the white ladies,—not Ysolt, is the virgin with lillies & a peacock receiving the divine messenger.

& then of course there are people in cities that are only 1/2 as high as they are & those by left of organ might have come from a greek vase

The last part of the journey was diversified by the wind. At first

non di più—qu'amas aura
Purg[10]

Then 'cui altra cura stringa'[11] so stiff as to be difficult to walk against.

TOULOUSE

And this church Vidal may well have known, the double colonnade that makes the nave seem narrow & leaves the transept for what it is a marvel of the Romanesque, mottled in colour & perfect.

It is I think the largest romanesque church I have seen & after San Zeno the finest.[12] Tho' it is wrong, perhaps, to compare them.

The Daurade, for this brick city by the greenish Garonne is also the city of Mandetta, the Daurade is ruined as utterly as a church can be. There remains of it nothing, nothing but the fine Roman proportion. Still is pleasant to be so near the scene of a perfectly constellated flirtation.

accordatta e stretta.[13]

For the bones of Clemence Isaure I care less
    they rest as they may & the flowers with them[14]

At mass the same clustering of stars about the altar, the same procession, the same movements of the cross & gold of the priest's garment, the same wind without the doors & the Garonne blown greyish

Pegulhan was of Tolosa

Apropos of the Tolosa troubadours, that is it may as well be apropos of them as of anything, it seems to me that the translations of canzoni even such canzoni as are good enough without their music, are for the most part dull & uninteresting because the translators themselves are ignorant of the finer points of the art & that being so they can not expect to convey to the reader the charm of the original. For the charm in poetry or in any other art is nothing else, & nothing less than the effect of the "finer points" which are for the most part amenable to law—tho' the sentimentalist & amateur would have us think for the most part, otherwise.

The Pyrenees

After his brief stopover in Toulouse, Pound took a night train south to Foix—gateway to the Pyrenees. He covered the seventy-odd kilometers between Foix and Axat on foot in two days, leaving the main road to clamber up to the hilltop ruins of the Cathar stronghold of Rocafixada. Pound's 1912 notes, however, indicate that he was still more or less oblivious to the Albigensian history of the Ariège. He walked within ten kilometers of Montségur and duly observed its dramatic perch "on its stilt of a mountain with a little snow behind it," but he clearly did not think the fortress worth the detour. It was only in the summer of 1919, while revisiting the Foix region with Dorothy in late June, that he first climbed up to its summit and deduced that it must have been some sort of "Cantabrian sun-temple"—"Mont Ségur, sacred to Helios" (87/588), solar omphalos of the later *Cantos.*

The evident impact of the Pyrenees on the traveler's imagist eye is also recorded by painterly vistas of "Provincia Deserta"—the first occurrence in Pound's poetry of that rarefied, virtually Chinese landscape of mountains and valleys which provides the elevated topography of the *paradiso* of the late *Cantos:*

> I have lain in Rocafixada,
> > level with sunset,
> Have seen the copper come down
> > tingeing the mountains,
> I have seen the fields, pale, clear as an emerald,
> Sharp peaks, high spurs, distant castles.
> I have said: "The old roads have lain here.
> Men have gone by such and such valleys
> Where the great halls were closer together."
> I have seen Foix on its rock . . .
> > > ("Provincia Deserta")

FOIX

To Foix by night, for here lived that count who wrote

"Mas qui a flor se vol meschlar"[1]

We are come again to a place where the waters run swiftly & where we have always this chinese background.

The faint grey of the mountains

The castle of Foix stands as everyone knows on a sharp little rock between the V of 2 rivers, perpendicular above its town & close to a baldish mountain this is shaped like the rump of a very thin, very great elephant[2] & below is fast water, & about are high hills, green, & light green & distant, & there you have it, three towers, a buttress & some bridges & red pink weeds by the wayside if you look back from the rd. to Quillan.

There was another sharp rock to build on but I dare say Foix is the strongest.

I had at last my plan of starting late in the day so the hills were full of cloud & mist & there were bright & dim colours upon them.

I went into this Coliseum of hills with Foix like Caesar's stand behind me, but with a veiled light over it & scarcely visible.

I went out the other end where a great sheet of rock juts thru the quarry, out & into a paler basin that faced me with light emerald & pearlish shadows.

Then you go up & over till the sky shows blue before you. It is not the rd. of the diligence.

One may lie on the earth & possess it & feel the world below one

I took the road again at Foix not from a sense of duty but from a wish to see some Pyrenees, some Pyrenees that is on this side of France, a wish shared by no known troubadour.

"To goon on pilgrimages" is a respectable & ancient habit, it implies a shrine, etc., but to go for mere mts. is decadent, I presume, & modern or at least parvenu & dating from the Ossianic movement.

Of course the quest of adventure is another matter, that also is respectably medieval, but I can not be said to be seeking adventure—a greatly overestimated commodity—for the pleasant ones one can never mention [marginal note: No gallantry in a land smelling of garlic. Impossible.] & the kind that make good telling are usually very fatiguing & uncomfortable while they last, & even then, if one plays anything like a role, a laudable role, this modern, false modern self consciousness keeps one from boasting of it. Assuredly

Foix.

Roquefixade.

Montségur.

adventure is of little use except to an author, & an author had much better pretend, pretend, I mean, that adventures befell John Donne or Giles Faring or whomsoever.

At any rate I am going the route in sheer truancy.

There is a Mauléon miles to the west which may or may not be *the* Mauléon[3]—at any rate it is said to be a dull place, & up by Castres lies Burlats with a pavilion à Adelaide, at east of it a little is Riquer St. Pons. St. Pons de Tournau [?], but I am heading for Carcassonne with which Troubadours had little to do, & I go by a route that presumably no jongleur ever bothered to climb.

Foix was very right to come to.

ROQUEFIXADE

I said this was a route without associations but after one has gone along a ledge of rd. beneath towers & fangs of rock & across a sort of open and up another incline one comes to Rocafixada. I see no reason why this should not have been the hold of a certain little known Q de R.

There is a huge sort of dorsal fin of rock that lifts sharp out of the mtn. One doubts if a man could climb it but there cradled in the sheer mad top of it are the ruins & the arches.

The sky is like a palmer's shell & the herd of hills lies before this.

I mounted the sheer face of rock to this castle & this was as I think of it one of the maddest things I have done in my life & of the sanest. There are chances to break one's neck not only in the ascent to the castle, but from this to the keep, & there in crevasses of ruin. & the land lies below darkening to copper, & the roads like white corals upon it.

Of this place there is nothing in the archives

walls of keep 12 ft. thick
went thru alcove of 7 5 ft walls. beyond it terrace. crevice of rock 2 ft. wide.
weakness–water suffering supply

Sky jap pink & grey when I descended other side—man & oxen. Béziers. S. at Toulouse.

& I went down the darkening valley, & behind me there was light at the base of the rock & the ruined wall acrest it, & I was perhaps foolish for there was an inn in that place & the people were kindly.

But I came down thru pine wood smelling of evening & few stars above me & the mts known only as shadow. O dies et candide lapis,[4] but it was a road to gallop not to walk on & the only sounds were me & a few tired crickets & one toad & the several dogs I waked, & gradually the sky brocaded itself, & near Lavalanet I met a mason who told me his troubles & so I finished that journey.

MONTSÉGUR

I set out the following day with the castle Montségur, which I had seen from before Roquefixade still in sight on its stilt of a mountain with a little snow behind it.[5] The road from Lavelanet lies thru the valley & is devilish hot of mornings with the sun in ones eyes, & the colour worth next to nothing & the flies thoroughly damnable. Were I possessed of any superabundance of common sense I should have waited for the diligence, for at least a part of the distance.

I held a late noon at Puivert, however, & proceeded at a saner hour. One comes to sharp green hummock of mountain with a false castle of its own rock but this is no second Fixada, tho' the pines may well give a green name to the peak here.

The fortress of Puivert is on an easy cone in the plateau beyond this, a stumpy keep, with the proper compliment of walls, 6 towers, square built like the Scaliger castles.[6]

The town is a remnant, completely hidden.

QUILLAN

Whether it is a haze of heat or whether it is only the effect of sunlight & of great distance, I do not know but there come with these mts, as the sun lowers, a colour at once metallic & oriental, as of a substance both dim & burnished.

Gaze on a mirrour & you will get something of the quality of colour, but here are many colours & the mirrour is deeper.

By 4:30 sky is a fine Saracenic blue with charred & blunted edges.

Above Quillan the rd. leads into Chinese unreality, we enter this & leave Puivert square upon the sky line behind us.

One should descend into Quillan by ladder, the rd. is a waste of time. But the great gates are before you & that may be held repayment.

Quillan has quiet waters & the square stump of a castle. My demons of energy & greed drove me thence straight on that night into Axat. This route is as famous as I am, but then what will you, the reputation is so much older?[7]

The sides of this pass rise higher than the buildings in Wall St. They are not unlike them in colour. It is true that they do not always rise so abruptly and that the gulch is not so narrow at bottom. Still as De Musset has so eloquently said "it is a fine sight for even a New Yorker." Our author is here violently wrong it was not De Musset but *Gautier*

"Ici l'impossible"[8]

It is a mad stack of sheets & sprires & obelisks, with a green mass of debris.

Some faces of the rocks are sheer as those of a building & some are low & jutting.

Dwarfed cedars clutch at the crevices at bottom the stream is almost as green as they are. There is a Chinese bridge of poles across this current.

AXAT

20 mi. below here is Pradas, but Daude from that place did not amount to much.[9] & beyond there is Figuera. but 2nd rate troubadours were scattered all over this land from Paris to Portugal. One cannot be bothered tracing all of them.

There was likewise a small Pegulhan, but that troubadour was of Tolosa. I have mention of him elsewhere (S.O.R.)[10]

Beyond St. Martin Lys is another less acute defile, a place more abounding in trees, the rock softer & more broken, the rd. winds thru' the rugged way of the opposing mts.

It is less Ming.

Less like a sport of gods & more like the work of nature.

Twas thru such a pine wood maybe that they hunted mad Peire Vidal. Smith puts Cabaret near Cabestang but I can not so find it.[11]

There seems to be no end to this & similar gorges but I stop at Axat.

47 k. since morning to my credit & the gorges of St. George before me.

The Languedoc Coast

From Axat, Pound caught a train to Peire Vidal's Carcassonne, where he stopped briefly before moving on by rail to Narbonne—whence he set off inland, walking across the marshes and dunes to Capestang, home of the troubadour Guilhem de Cabestang (whose grisly fate is rehearsed in Canto 4). The next day, still recovering from the heat, he passed through Béziers and made his way along the Canal du Midi to the coastal resort town of Agde. The following morning he was off to Arles by train.

Pound's initial impressions of the torrid Mediterranean coast, so hastily jotted down as to be almost illegible, bespeak a mood whose uncharacteristic autobiographical explicitness has clearly been heightened by heat and exhaustion. The lineation of the small notebook he kept during this portion of his trip has been retained in order to convey the rhythms of what nearly reads like a stream of consciousness in enjambed *vers libre*.

CARCASSONNE

[missing pages]
The way to have painted this properly was—but he died [illegible] in the year before our Xtn grace—, with the works unattempted, so the gentle reader must go south and do his own gazing. And you must not go by train for the train goes thru a little black hole not so large as my lady's parlour, & you will see nothing at all from the windows.

Carcassonne was as we all know overflowed by a mass of inertia which has preserved it as has the lava Pompeii. From the walls one looks out to Pennautier which may have been Loba's.[1]

NARBONNE AND BÉZIERS

Shell
like the cities

Cité de Carcassonne.

Carcassonne.

in tapestry
beyond the vineyards
new slate
personal note
only in ruin of hall, the
trace of some
intimate usage,
an occasional pillar
of a window,
high in thick wall
where time &
hands have not
reached it.

the further the
more like
legends

Too like
the roofs over
Regents Park
or St. Jane,
bright, & as light
utter magic
Low ridge of
hills grey
in a mist
of heat
to Narbonne.

Narbonne
Per la glori del terraine
A la memori
De la vescontessa
n' Ermengarda XIIeme
et dels trobadors
Benrhart Alan han
Gui. Fabre XIIIeme
G. Riquier
filhs glorios de
Narbona la arrada[2]

Narbonne is not so bad
as they say it is
—baking hot
but not so dull
as they say it is.[3]
Despite an entrance like second
rate Paris, or like
any middle western town
you observe. —No,
this place has its charm.
It does as well as any
if one would sit in a
wide café and read
De Maupassant. I came
to weep the departed
sea coast, but Narbonne is
still maritime,—or
scant pretenses, a
brown canal of boats
& washerwomen, a
washed out face of
Venice,—but no,
here is colour, a bridge
of houses & the biggest of
them bright, & a strong pinkish.
It is the Latin touch that moves me?
Possibly.
The court of the
municipio let us call it
& its tablet, no longer
gallic.
          ‹qt.›
The medieval church,
with buttress & battlements
is "late" but hang it all
one can not forever play philologist.
This place had an
epic also—which is
out of the picture, a
chançon de geste, so
let us digress a
while.

Gallia Narbonensis.[4]

Narbonne-Capestang
It is strange to find
oneself walking on the
flat after one has
grown used to ruts.
But there was a certain friendliness in
the rd. as I set out
from Narbonne that evening.
First with the speckled banks
of the sycamores beside
me, then with scrub wall, &
then where the dunes begin,
a land of vine
& olives,
olive trees when
one has been nearly a yr. out
of Italy, that
is enough to pay one in a day
[deleted: for false friends
& lying reviewers],
as hills rise
beyond this plane,
faint as a
cloud of dust.
To the left is
a ruined castle of
the marshes, &
what might be Cabestang.[5]
a guisa de leon[6]
        q.s.p.
half high in the
middle distance.

Out of the Aude
into Hérault.[7]

The sun was
in its clouds
like a pink
paper lantern,

& whether it was
that I was
very tired,
or whether it was in the
temper of air
or the lay
of the land
here,
this walk
was like
a coming home,
one expected half . . to
meet with one's
people.
The boy with the
sheep loitered
as if he knew
me, & wanted me
to talk.
Capestang is—
as the name indicates etc.
Here is a castle
that really
hangs lights in
its towers
or rather it was
only a ruined church
that looked like a
castle in the darkness,
but I was too tired
to mind the difference.

& I assure you
that veal stew with
carrots & olives
together is a dish
most excellent.

At about 8 miles
from here, west, is Montoulier,
perhaps the Montaussier of Tibors[8]
but I turned east, to Béziers.

The next day it
was too hot to move
so I sent my clothing
to the canal &
awaited the sun set.
But it was a cool autobus that
rescued me at 5.
(the poor ruin of Chat. does not
show above the
houses).

The land to the
west with the halation of
dust & heat,
still keeps the
illusion &
shows the
seas work upon it.
There is a stiff
tower on the sand—
head of Montady.
As for Béziers,
the town
is undeniably &
irremediably hideous. The
river is its one
extenuation.
Strong it
undoubtedly was,
& its viscount a
person of some
consequence.[9]
Approaching, one
sees a wall
in disadornment
& a hulk of a
church across it
& from there
the plain
lies before one
& some where
out upon & beyond it,

the one point of possible
interest, the [illegible].
The church is
machicolei &
battlement but
not much,
even so, to look at.
It combines
the disadvantages
of today & those of
the mid-ages,
all of them.

And these things
being so, I
came to rest
that night at
the hotel of the White Horse
upon the Quai in Agde.
I came here
along the canal,
under a mediterranean
sky, ah
surely I know
my métier, there
are artists in
other media
but when it
comes to living I
know my métier.
I have made horrible
mistakes, I have
lived thru horrible
things—but horrible—
but still I know
métier, as perhaps no one
since Flaccus[10]
has known it.

Can a man
be bothered making
poetry of nights like
this! Fools, readers of books,

go south & live
there. It is
all I have to
say for this time
to the end of it,
that life,
despite all
its damnable
tangles & circumformations
is worth the candle,
go south & live there
days nights &
the rest of it, in
body or in spirit.
Cueillez! Carpe
and the rest of it,
raris, the day, &
the colour, &
the sound, the
hour, or what thing
or things, is
most or
mostly
near to the heart—
or your desire!
But be
not cheap or
mediocre in
desiring. Almost, not
quite, I was quoting Baudelaire's
Be drunken.[11]
I who have lived 4 mos at a stretch
in Venice, & twice
for weeks and months on end
in Sirmio "venusta,"[12]
shall I break
into dithyrambs for one
night, on a
quai in a forgotten
city. Because
there is a little
water under my
window

& the sky is of a reasonable
complexion?

On one side
the sea bleached &
colourless, on the
other the Etang de Thau deep
blue as if
seen thru
a frosted pane.

Arles, Nîmes, Beaucaire

Pound spent the next week in the valley of the Rhône, visiting Arles, Nîmes, and the twin town of Beaucaire/Tarascon, resting up from his journey and recasting his travel notes into more definitive form. Of these three towns, it was Arles that spoke most deeply to his literary imagination. The Romanesque cloister of St. Trophime, the Roman amphitheater, the ancient burial ground of Aliscamps mentioned by Dante in the *Inferno*—all return in various shades of gray in his later poetry.

While in Arles, Pound corrected the proofs for his "Psychology and Troubadours," later included in *The Spirit of Romance*. His observations on the Latin sensuality of the city bear out his contention in that essay that "Provençal song is never wholly disjunct from the pagan rites of May Day." (SOR, 90). But whereas "Psychology and Troubadours" emphasized an art of *trobar clus* based on the sublimation of sexuality into a neo-Platonic "cult of Amor," the pagan spectacle of Arles proposed a Dionysian immediacy of gratification that obviously struck an ambivalent chord in Pound's still uncertain sense of eros and identity.

The imposing tower of Beaucaire, which overlooks the river Rhône across from the town of Tarascon (so affectionately described in Ford Madox Ford's *Provence*) later provided the stage-setting for the surge of medieval pageantry on the first page of Ur-Canto I. Attempting to move beyond "th'intaglio method" of his Imagist verse, Pound parodies Browning's *Sordello* as he casts about for a modern poetics more adequate to the epic resurrection of the past as *"our* life, your life, my life, extended":

> Tower by tower
> Red-brown the rounded bases, and the plan
> Follows the builder's whim. Beaucaire's slim gray
> Leaps from the stubby base of Altaforte—
> Mohammed's windows, for the Alcazar
> Has such a garden, split by a tame small stream.
> The moat is ten yards wide, the inner courtyard
> Half a-swim with mire.
> Trunk hose?
> > There are not. The rough men swarm out
> In robes that are half Roman, half like the Knave of Hearts:
> And I discern your story:
> > > (P,229)

ARLES

Across the pavement Dante's footsteps had followed those of Frederick Barbarossa.[1] 1st the man of action, then the theorist, the one to receive a crown,
the other to crown the city with a phrase at random

"si com ad Arli"[2]

Arles reveals so much—around you Arles is a city, is not a country to be
walked across or a mt. you can climb to the top of.
   . . . There are machines, there are ghosts & corpses of cities, all of them,
but no, Arles is the other sort, the living complex—like Venice, or Verona, or
perhaps Cadiz, even tho I throw in this last as a mere venture.
   You can not in any real sense *see* such places, you pass & you return, & you
know like fate in the weaving that some time you will come back for good
there, for a time that is, for a liason, for this is in the run what it comes to, a
satiation, a flowing out from yourself into the passion & mood of the complex.
   Then are there cities that are passionate in their personal hold upon us. You
may play the string as you like. It is not the bath of the crowd, it is different,
it is the place, the place that made the people, it is seductive as the creative
principle is always seductive, it touches or it clings and we go out & through
& into it, and are one with it, infused & inflowing.

The air. The sun. The wind.
   & the stars above the city.

———

   Les Aliscamps

what a place to
hold witches sabbath,
the double tombs,
deep for 2,

what vividness
Io credo al ginochhi
levata[3]

shallow with
head holes,
dens of beasts. etc.

more numerous &
vary.
open & lidless.[4]

ARLES: THE *PASSEO*[5]

Here Poetry would not be of the Art at all, but a part of life. Like, one might say, the private house decoration. —No, rather like a part of the tribal marriage customs—at one remove from the dance. "lou soleu me fai cantar" (motto, Hotel Forum) that is decorated out of Mistral.[6] These people actually "sing" "trobar" in the natural course of things. What the dance is to the savage here, in the natural course of things in this system of the *passeo*, a harem system where the women are regularly paraded without veils, a gay irresponsible-seeming, hide-bound system, the made song would have its part. So Arles explains so much, so much why the great mass of Provençal canzons are what they are, why the whole thing "l'amour courtois" & the rest of it was just what it was & why there is no use trying to find subtle under- or over currents. —Save perhaps in the works of an occasional exception, possibly in an Arnaut, and then later & certainly in that other school which was so wholly different[7] & even there it is the individual not the school to whom such things may be attributed.

The people may be as they are here charming & gay & bent on an innocent but un-intellectual pleasure, but subtleties & austerities of the mind are never to their vogue or their liking, either here or elsewhere—where this sensuous life is less charming & there is perhaps an end to the whole matter. The sensuous inconsequent-consequent life is beautiful where the sun makes it so. Is beautiful where bodies & plumage are beautiful, where gaiety & pride are mingled to make it so, & it is unconditionally hideous under an evil climate or where warped or stretched to a motive.

To a sane intellectual or even northern audience the first need of poetry is that it be good poetry. But to this comfortable, intelligent, brainless, thoroughly sexual audience who can not always be dancing the Zarrabondilla—to whom the Zarrabondilla is probably denied altogether, the first need is that speech be poetry, I mean that it take the place of dancing.[8]

What to "us" is art, is *maestria*, "monumentum perennis" and so on, & aimed at eternity must here be aimed at no such elusive target. No! the proper goal is next evening, or failing that, a month, or a year's time—this last as heroism and demonic patience.

And the theatre for all this: the grey, beautiful city, is as appropriate or as

Arles. The Cloister of Saint Trophime.

Beaucaire. Le Château.

unappropriate as if it all took place in the actual ruin of the Roman play-
house, life or the pagan gods in all their bravura, overflows the ruin of all
things made & arranged in pattern or in an order contrived.

The grey stone is darker than the grey of Paris, Versailles, Fontainebleau,
where everything was plotted and contrived as a background for bright trivial
figures out of Watteau.

It was not for nothing that Dante thought of the Aliscamps in his Inferno.
The iron is in the colour. Of Rome indeed there is much here, & what the
middle ages made of their Roman ruins is left for us to guess, for they say very
little about them & set them for the most part to some strange & practical
uses. To serve that is for defences & churches & stables.

The walls express the republic & Dante who had seen them with the arena
for 2^{nds} might well sneer at the [illegible].
   Inferno. Amphitheatre
   Arles.   Verona.[9]

      Greece & Orient
         in Provence[10]

NÎMES

Nîmes has opened itself over reasonable space. The streets are wide, there is
plenty of air & room to move in.

A certain number of very neat roman remains are disposed in a conven-
tional part of a gleaming modern city. Nîmes is in broad U.S. a good town,
perhaps not so "good" as Cincinnati or St. Louis, but the water is brought
you iced in a carafe, the ice cream is passable, & served for example, in
respectable quantities. Apart from these advantages, the people do not look
interesting, they are probably all right but they will have bull fights.

A pleasing bit of new Paris with certain very neat railroad most neatly
dispersed about it. A good town in broad U.S., better than Buffalo not quite
so good as Cincinnati.

But this bull fight is not against them, if they are all as mild as the affair of
July 12, 1912.

First they let loose some pigeons, then they let go some fireworks, then
they let out a bull with padded horns, and when he was tired he scrambled
over the bull with consumate grace & ease.

BEAUCAIRE

I find among someone's notes the following chapts.

Memory is an odd thing, it happens to me & I suppose it happens to others. That a certain portion of my life has befallen me, me, myself in a certain intimate way, & much more of it has happened about me, has fallen upon a sort of penumbra, with which I have little or no concern.

Certain things happen & continue, they exist in us by a species of recurrence, they fall vividly into our days & nights after they are in one sense over & done with.

And there are other things, often "more important" often more seemingly vital which pass into a sort of unreality & seem like a dream or fiction.

And there are certain other events which seem only to flow about us.[11]

And finding these things so, seeing in a way how many persons may flow thru us or flow past us while we are alive, while we are as animals enjoying our individual & continuous existence one is tempted to wonder what final part this cell or trait of memory should play, or is to play in our vaunted immortality, in our cycle of recurrence.

And perhaps our individuality, or name of name, is a finer & more durable thing than this childish trick of remembering.

Perhaps we exist as the notes of the string exist, for a

is always an

whoever or whatever strikes it. And tho' it is in a sense the same it is different on different instruments & perhaps our sequence of lives has this in common with the music that we [are] struck upon divers times & give sounds of diverse timbre in response to the striking.

With the stars at Beaucaire above me I begin this transcription.

TARASCON

Tarascon
Richartz,

strong tower
but over against it
is Beaucaire & it is the
world wide knowledge
it was of Beaucaire
of a goodly castle
& some say this
Beaucaire was on sea
evaso.

Arles, still port,
mediterranean difference &
etc.

Beaucaire from Tarascon.
The town named for
its tower,[12] & it
is well fitting
for it is I think the finest castle I
have ever seen, & perfectly
fits the legend,
the [illegible] down beside the
cliff, etc.
More than
one house with its Tower
& battlement—the stage setting absolutely
implies it
the thing is
geomorphic.

St. Marthan
holy ground
Clodovic circa 500
& rewarded
Tarascon

If there were ever
a town made to
pitch a romance
in, it is Beaucaire,
the very place
a Saracen captive
would be.

Long stair
after port-cullis
& bare of rocks.

romanesque
early carving
of small tower
exquisite

Tarascon, new,
the flat
land the
barrier against
the sea.
The sweep
of the valley.
Alluvion of the Rhone.

gt.   △   keep

dungeon in base
of tower,
accessible
on next outer
range of rampart.

land absolutely
flat, with hills.
flat winding Rhone.

Tarascon dwarfed
from the keep:
stalls, under port-
cullis, ecurie
outside

Shell—rest
destroyed by Richelieu in
disgusting feud[13]
just enough
rooms left—
to be fascinating,

little window
with seat by it
in top room
of keep, on right—there
should be of such things
only one.
Beyond keep
signs of a
garden of trees

Foundation Roman or
small my guesses.

Let it stand in
proof of my sanity—
despite all
opinions gainst it
that I spent a week in Beaucaire,
I wrote a great slice of this book
there

The Auvergne

The final leg of Pound's walking tour took him through the Auvergne—the volcanic landscape of the troubadours Guilhem de Saint-Didier, Peire Cardinal, Peire d'Auvergne, Peire Rogier, and Peire de Maensac (whose *vida* is retold in "Provincia Deserta" and in Cantos 5 and 23). Catching a train from Tarascon, Pound traveled northward to Le Puy and covered the remaining 150 kilometers to Clermont-Ferrand on foot in the space of four or five days. Traversing the high plateau of the Vélay, he skirted the castle of Polignac, stopped at the ruins of Allègre, and then moved on north to the great Benedictine monastery at Chaise-Dieu. At Chaise-Dieu, he turned eastward and climbed through the steep woodland to Champagnac, before dropping down into the valley of the Allier river, which he then followed north in the rain all the way to Clermont. On the outskirts of the city, he ran into a band of Gypsies: Pound's irritable record of this encounter in his walking tour notes is at considerable variance with the picaresque bonhomie he conjures up in his 1915 poem "The Gypsy" (APP 2).

LE PUY

I was wondering how I should extricate my self from Tarascon and prepare myself, or my canvas for a new place if you will, for a new city of "20,793" inhabitants, but my train comfortably derailed a part of itself and I found myself at some junction or other with no train connection for hours & an autobus at my disposal. And twenty miles of mountain air, & of conversation with the curé of X washed free my mind of its preoccupation, & I entered Le Puy by way of Taulhac. As Smith has described the paysage, I shall not attempt it, save to say that after the other valley that of Le Puy was little alluring.[1] One sees that city sprawled about two rusty spikes of rock & the Tower of Puy on a similar pedestal beyond it. And the yellow slab sides of houses & the brick coloured roofs were very ugly. And I detest colored statues.

As for the cathedral its colour distresses one.[2] A church may be striped but should not be speckled & it was a great mistake to change the stair colour. After the exquisite grey of Arles one can not do with it, the grey in the cloister of S. Trophime.

---

colossal statues, especially colour of yellow terra cotta

Church striped as in northern Italy or Mosque in Cordova. Interior not exterior.

St. Michael is decorated in the taste of Tibet.[3] It is also speckled but it is too small for this to matter. The shape is the shape of the rock. The view to the east is passable. Place swarms with beggars & women wanting to sell one lace. Good fast aeroplane doing the circuit.

ALLÈGRE

Gui St. Leidier was doubtless a man of exquisite & polished manners but his poetry does not interest me.

As for Polignac, the sum of his amours, it rests now a solid tower on a very solid rock. The data are in Smith,[4] & the present prioress is or was a year or so ago among the most noted ornaments of the field.

It will be seen from this that I am walking from Le Puy to Clermont for the sake of the open country rather than for that of auld acquaintances.

The prince of Croy is by the way an "héritier" of the late king of the Belges. There goes another illusion.

Before noon I found myself in St. Paulien where I had not intended to come at the outset & at 2:15 in Allègre. The colour of the hill was for the most part uninteresting or repugnant but it is pleasant to walk thru crumpled pine wood & in one place flat to the sky line. A square field of bachelor's buttons but it's more vivid here, the 1/2 cycle of hill far behind it.

The church at St. Paulien is a curious shape & the lighting of the apse is beautiful.

On first seeing Allègre back of the Mt. Du Bar one thinks the tower bridge has slipped its moorings by some freak of gravitation, a free bridge of battlements still standing connects two of the fragments. The arch is well concealed.

There is a great lake of landscape beneath this portal & the P.M. haze had mellowed it. The town is apparently built of cobble stones & would be amazing had not one seen Uzerche.

	Allègre
? curious carving	the joyous
39 story fire-place	[illeg]
same date as Le Puy	machicolée

Allègre.

The "Gallows" of Allègre.

9th cent. or 14th   in trefoil

style–stone?

                                        or
                                  clumsy masonry
                                      stone here
                                      so hard!

July 16
4.04 P.M.
now should I be finally equipped for the indicting of true pastorals

        •
      • •   called Allègre
      Rossinhols[5]   in Limoge

Spurt –wurt
even the dilettante reviewers
know   spear it
                near it

CHAISE-DIEU

The approach to Chaise Dieu lies thru a wide hell of timber pine. The ruin is stupendous & too much hidden by houses & fairly reeks with history which the benevolent reader is just as well able to look up in the encyclopedia as I am (it is outside the circus of this narration).

The tapestries are the finest I have seen bar those in the Musée de Cluny.[6]

Rose garden might be Roman de la Rose not so grand as Virgin in the garden da Verona by Stefano da Verona of that city.[7]

Bulk of abbey seems to crush out the town, as one looks back at it from rd. to St. Germain-L'Herm.

As this said rd. to l'Herm was almost impossible to find & quite impossible to follow finally found myself well along another & came so into Champagnac & to Auzon. In Champagnac by a shelf of rd. where the gulf lay next it and where the further mts. lay beyond in chiffon.

If any one care for that conglomeration of different coloured humps which the vulgar term mtn. scenery let him try Auvergne. There is a hellish climb before one gets to Champagnac

& then a sunblazed world lies under one
1st near. 2nd far.
Champaganc itself was clogged with a fair of bulls, bullocks, bull calves
apparently as stupid as their owners.

Gendarme
   ? sell scapulaires

at Chastrette	knows
1st gleam of the Allier	what the
like a minor	sea-bottom
scale	looks like
quick air	down hill
	from
mts.? 90 m.	here

bowls for gold fish decoration

THE ALLIER

Jumeaux. K. 46–7.
   There being no visible reason for staying in Auzon I moved forward to
Jumeaux
   I should have [gone?] to Saut du Loup.
   This day I went thru a valley full of castles, important castles & small
towns & progress of the sordid sort.
   The last diverting day of my travels? Perhaps because my mind was
already before me, already full of London & Paris. —Not that I was tired of
vagabondage for once caught the fever returns & I had already planned
another excursion & peribasis.
   At Le Breuil certain members of the next generation were busy with soap
bubbles. I have to report that soap bubbles are in this region blown not from
clay pipes but from straws.

   Having sat for a while on one of the stone guards of a bridge wall near
Issoire the air being still damp with rain could not say that the day was
wasted.

   Chateau at Issoire, interesting—moorish,—zodiac on east of multiplied
apses—outer color—mellowed.

With Le Pin came an improvement.

The muddy Allier is the least inspiring of all the rivers I had come upon.

Over against Coudes was Le Buron, a hold of the counts of Auvergne & there now hung like a torn rag in the remnant of the storm

Vs. Parent great oblong black stump hardly to be distinguished from the rock that is its base.

Coudes is not unpleasant.

The commune forbids itself to "bohémiens"

Above Coudes the rd. mounts & the way begins to be worth walking.

A storm is about to gather

& so on & so on until I found myself in the restaurant of Hugo which is a good 33 m. from Jumeaux. Journeys end in divers fashions.

This is my longest tramp but I believe with American boots & a little practice & a reasonably constructed pack a man might do 50 m. per day & enjoy it.

And so on & so on. Clermont not a bad sight, but the climax of the trip had come 6 m. without the city

A rain storm not the one I have mentioned but another which displayed the full resources of the country had refreshed all my forces.

I was making at least 6 k. per hr. & about 9 in spurts & was already feeling in fair fettle but I nearly burst with RAGE when a strapping gipsy who was leading a monkey & an ape stopped & asked me if I had seen "autres des camarades avec des ours et des singes."

   Sanguine [illegible]
    vs. bloody rage

Clermont	Paris
21.45	
9:45 P.M.	5.40
8.50 A.M.	5.45 P.M.

the mist clots about the trees in the valley

the gt. drops of mtn. rain break thru the heat about me

The smoky Clermont was not a bad sight itself with the sun above it

FRAGMENTS FROM *GIRONDE*

Fragments from *Gironde*

The first of these fragments intended for *Gironde* is included among the handwritten papers of the *Walking Tour* at Beinecke Library and bears the title "Chapt. IV (or V)." Before veering off into a philippic against American magazine editors, it sketches out an essay on the craft of Provençal rhyme. The second fragment, entitled "The Normal Opportunity of the Provençal Troubadour," is a typescript contained in folder 5159 of the Pound Archive. It was probably written in late 1912 or early 1913—somewhere between the composition of *Gironde* and the publication of "Troubadours: Their Sorts and Conditions" (*Quarterly Review*, Oct. 1913), of which it would appear to be an early draft.

CHAP. IV (or V)

The reason why Provençal canzos are for the most part deadly dull in translation are not far to seek. I shall try to illustrate by this canzo of Peire Vidal which is in some ways easy, in some ways very difficult to render.

This chapter is purely technical & the general reader may as well skip it.

Ab l'alen[1]

to follow the rime scheme one may begin as follows

> Breathing do I draw toward me
> Air that comes from where Provence is
> All that comes from there entrances
> me so that when they accord me
>
> news of it, for all I am told
> I cry for a hundred fold
> So love I the tidings of it

& this version has the faults of 90 + 9 just versions of Provençal canzos.

Rime does not consist in merely matching terminations.

Vidal here uses -aire, -ensa, -en, -ire.
I have given illustration of the value of this sort of blending in a canzo which
has no other value save that it sings to its tune & can serve as example,
    -aces -aneth -aideth -azes
of this sort of modulation.[2]

One may try the translation again.

> news, I laugh & call again
> give ten hundred words for ten

> So doth speech of it restore me

It is not yet very good but this will serve but the better to illustrate that the
charm of a short rimed lyric of this sort lies largely in a felicitous modulation
of the rime sounds.
    That rime is not enough.
    Now any ass can rime & Gascoigne long since pointed out that if you start
thus the alphabet,
                    at, bat, cat, bog, clog, frog,
you can easily & speedily rime whenever you choose.[3]
    It should be sufficiently apparent that this trick requires no special genius,
& it should be by now sufficiently recognized that if a man rimes he must
rime in an interesting manner.
    I do not mean by this an excentric or startling or noticibly novel manner.
Mr. Yeats rimes finely with the simplest of means,
vid.

> Rose on tree of time

-ays -etc.[4]
It is done with male rime in couplet, in the simplest of arrangement with the
most perfect of modulation, & it is probable that he does it by "feel" rather
than theorem
    & Maurice Hewlett rimes well in the stricter forms, as in the
                    lai Gaubertz[5]
using harsh rimes & striking them smartly. Tho this manner would not fit
many modes or minds, & he here comes nearest to the tang of such Provençal
doubles as *atge*, for the teeth grip the sound & shake it.

& if I have done anything it is in "Autet."[6] Tho the rimes on 2 words in that canzo are bad & are only a makeshift to reproduce the effect of the Provençal feminine.

––––––––––

All these remarks are only given as hints that the English rimario is not yet exhausted and it is not my wish, tho it probably be a result of that chapter that in 1974 the editors of the Atlantic Monthly will write to the rising generation that their rimes lack acuteness & Piddlington of the Punch will write to Billy's grand nephew that his alcaics show paucity of rime & so & so of Scribbler will write to John Doe that his verses interest them very much but that he'll have to modulate if he wants to make a commercial success of them. An example given by an artist as good or bad under certain peculiar circumstances, & they make a rule of thumb & misapply it.

For all editors especially all American Editors are asses & they will lie then as they lie now for they will not care about any of these things. What they will want is slush & cheap optimism & evasion of life. & they always do want it.

And by evasion of life I include sham vigour & red blood & generalities about human brotherhood couched in undigested language.

& they will quote Southey & Lewis Morris.[7]

Axiom: all editors that are not by nature & intention essentially base, do by continued practice of their trade become so.

Axiom: there is not & never can be a truce between the living art & the magazines, tho there may under exceptional circumstances be a lull of hostilities.

Yet there are certain places where editors are not yet sufficiently despised. Lux fiat, as the first step toward the liberation of our art.

THE NORMAL OPPORTUNITY OF
THE PROVENÇAL TROUBADOUR

More than once, when I have spoken about the mediaeval Provençals, I have been asked about the sources of our knowledge of them. Besides a few text-books and reprints, there are numerous manuscripts, on parchment, illumi-nated, for the most part folios, the greater number in Paris at the National Library and at the library of the Arsenal, the rest scattered in the Vatican, the Ambrosiana at Florence [*sic*] and the other libraries of Europe.[8] Few of these were written earlier than the 14th century. A small percentage of them contain musical notation, and these latter are very important, for few Provençal *canzoni* are good enough to stand without their tunes. I do not mean, of necessity, that the rest are bad *canzoni*, but that poems made to be sung must be judged by a standard very different from that whereby we judge a poem made to be spoken or read. It must be remembered also that these *canzoni* were sung one or two at a time; they were not intended to be heard or read in bulk.

There are three ways of "going back," of feeling as well as knowing about the troubadours, first, by way of the music, second, by way of the land, third, by way of the books themselves, for a manuscript on vellum has a sort of life and personality which no work of the press attains.[9] The Ambrosian library possesses a MS (R71 superiore), a thoroughbred, with clearly written words and music, which contains the extant tunes of Arnaut Daniel. Another MS (Fonds fr. 20050) in the Bibliothèque Nationale at Paris, a small quarto with music, is so very old that it might have been carried by some late singer on the road; while Ms. fr. 856 is fat, like a dictionary and was certainly made for reading. And there is Ms. fr 844, the courtly book in which the authors are arranged by rank and precedence: Anjou, Navarre, the Canon, the Chastelaine, Sire Morisses de Creon, Gilles de Beaumont with his hand on his heart—for they are all pictured in the capitals with their arms and blazons—Jehans de Louvois with his lance, Couci with rabbits in the margin, Mesire Bouchers de Malli, proper nights all, and Tiebaus de Blason. It is a book to set young girls thinking, for surely we have all this array to show us that a tempting singer need not lack of necessity goods lands and houses.[10] Ms. fr 854 is among the most clearly written and contains the *razzos*, or notes of biography and explanation. From it I quote or abridge the great part of what follows.[11]

We are perhaps too apt to think of the troubadour as a person in mediaeval clothing, walking about on air to find sea-coasts in Bohemia or princesses in Tripoli, or suffering amorous mishap and ending, with his heart in my lady's pastry, as did literally poor Guillaume de Cabestang. But these things were no more the habit of the twelfth century than is motor banditage the habit of our own, and I have sought in the following excerpts to show what I shall call the "normal opportunity" of *jongleurs* and troubadours. I omit the best-known and more romantic tales.[12]

APPENDIX 1

TROUBADOURS: THEIR SORTS AND CONDITIONS

The argument whether or no the troubadours are a subject worthy of study is an old and respectable one. If Guillaume, Count of Peiteus, grandfather of King Richard Cœur de Leon, had not been a man of many energies, there might have been little food for this discussion. He was, as the old book says of him, "of the greatest counts in the world, and he had his way with women." He made songs for either them or himself or for his more ribald companions. They say that his wife was Countess of Dia, "fair lady and righteous," who fell in love with Raimbaut d'Aurenga and made him many a song. Count Guillaume brought composition in verse into court fashions, and gave it a social prestige which it held till the crusade of 1208 against the Albigenses. The mirth of Provençal song is at times anything but sunburnt, and the mood is often anything but idle. De Born advises the barons to pawn their castles before making war, thus if they won they could redeem them, if they lost the loss fell on the holder of the mortgage.

The forms of this poetry are highly artificial, and as artifice they have still for the serious craftsman an interest, less indeed than they had for Dante, but by no means inconsiderable. No student of the period can doubt that the involved forms, and the veiled meanings in the "trobar clus," grew out of living conditions, and that these songs played a very real part in love intrigue and in the intrigue preceding warfare. The time had no press and no theatre. If you wish to make love to women in public, and out loud, you must resort to subterfuge; and Guillaume St. Leider even went so far as to get the husband of his lady to do the seductive singing.

If a man of our time be so crotchety as to wish emotional, as well as intellectual, acquaintance with an age so out of fashion as the twelfth century, he may try in several ways to attain it. He may read the songs themselves from the old books—from the illuminated vellum—and he will learn what the troubadours meant to the folk of the century just after their own. He will learn a little about their costume from the illuminated capitals. Or he may try listening to the words with the music, for, thanks to Jean Beck and others,[1] it is now possible to hear the old tunes. They are perhaps a little Oriental in feeling, and it is likely that the spirit of Sufism is not wholly absent from their content. Or, again, a man may walk the hill roads and river roads from Limoges and Charente to Dordogne and Narbonne and learn a little, or more than a little, of what the country meant to the wandering singers, he may

[1] Walter Morse Rummel's *Neuf Chansons de Troubadours*, pub. Augener, Ltd., etc; also the settings by Aubry.

learn, or think he learns, why so many canzos open with speech of the weather; or why such a man made war on such and such castles. Or he may learn the outlines of these events from the "razos," or prose paragraphs of introduction, which are sometimes called "lives of the troubadours." And, if he have mind for these latter, he will find in the Bibliothèque Nationale at Paris the manuscript of Miquel de la Tour, written perhaps in the author's own handwriting; at least we read "I Miquel de la Tour, scryven, do ye to wit."

Miquel gives us to know that such and such ladies were courted with greater or less good fortune by such and such minstrels of various degree, for one man was a poor vavassour, and another was King Amfos of Aragon; and another, Vidal, was son of a furrier, and sang better than any man in the world; and Raimon de Miraval was a poor knight that had but part of a castle; and Uc Brunecs was a clerk and he had an understanding with a *borgesa* who had no mind to love him or to keep him, and who became mistress to the Count of Rodez. "Voila l'estat divers d'entre eulx."

The monk, Gaubertz de Poicebot, "was a man of birth; he was of the bishopric of Limozin, son of the castellan of Poicebot. And he was made monk when he was a child in a monastery, which is called Sain Leonart. And he knew well letters, and well to sing and well *trobar*.[1] And for desire of woman he went forth from the monastery. And he came thence to the man to whom came all who for courtesy wished honour and good deeds—to Sir Savaric de Mauleon—and this man gave him the harness of a joglar and a horse and clothing; and then he went through the courts and composed and made good canzos. And he set his heart upon a donzella gentle and fair and made his songs of her, and she did not wish to love him unless he should get himself made a knight and take her to wife. And he told En Savaric how the girl had refused him, wherefore En Savaric made him a knight and give him land and the income from it. And he married the girl and held her in great honour. And it happened that he went into Spain, leaving her behind him. And a knight out of England set his mind upon her and did so much and said so much that he led her with him, and he kept her long time his mistress and then let her go to the dogs (malamen anar). And En Gaubertz returned from Spain, and lodged himself one night in the city where she was. And he went out for desire of woman, and he entered the *alberc* of a poor woman; for they told him there was a fine woman within. And he found his wife. And when he saw her, and she him, great was the grief between them and great shame. And he stopped the night with her, and on the morrow he went forth with her to a nunnery where he had her enter. And for this grief he ceased to sing and to compose." If you are minded, as Browning was in his *One Word More*, you

[1] Poetical composition, literally "to find."

may search out the song that En Gaubertz made, riding down the second time from Malleon, flushed with the unexpected knighthood.

> Per amor del belh temps suau
> E quar fin amor men somo.[1]

"For love of the sweet time and soft" he beseeches this "lady in whom joy and worth have shut themselves and all good in its completeness" to give him grace and the kisses due to him a year since. And he ends in envoi to Savaric.

> Senher savaric larc e bo
> Vos troba hom tota fazo
> Quel vostre ric fag son prezan
> El dig cortes e benestan.[2]

La Tour has given us seed of drama in the passage above rendered. He has left us also an epic in his straightforward prose. "Piere de Maensac was of Alverne (Auvergne) a poor knight, and he had a brother named Austors de Maensac, and they both were troubadours and they both were in concord that one should take the castle and the other the *trobar*." And presumably they tossed up a *marabotin* or some such obsolete coin, for we read, "And the castle went to Austors and the poetry to Piere, and he sang of the wife of Bernart de Tierci. So much he sang of her and so much he honoured her that it befell that the lady let herself go gay (*furar a del*). And he took her to the castle of the Dalfin of Auvergne, and the husband, in the manner of the golden Menelaus, demanded her much, with the church to back him and with the great war that they made. But the Dalfin maintained him (Piere) so that he never gave her up. He (Piere) was a straight man (*dreitz om*) and good company, and he made charming songs, tunes and the words, and good coblas of pleasure." And among them is one beginning

> Longa saison ai estat vas amor
> Humils e francs, y ai faich son coman.[3]

Dante and Browning have created so much interest in Sordello that it may not be amiss to give the brief account of him as it stands in a manuscript in the Ambrosian library at Milan. "Lo Sordels *si fo di Mantovana*. Sordello was of

---

[1] For love of the fair time and soft,
  And because fine love calls me to it.
[2] Milord Savaric, generous
  To thy last bond, men find thee thus,
  That thy rich acts are food for praise
  And courtly are thy words and days.
[3] For a long time have I stood toward Love
  Humble and frank, and have done his commands.

Mantuan territory of Sirier (this would hardly seem to be Goito), son of a poor cavalier who had name Sier Escort (Browning's El Corte), and he delighted himself in chançons, to learn and to make them. And he mingled with the good men of the court. And he learned all that he could and he made coblas and sirventes. And he came thence to the court of the Count of St Bonifaci, and the Count honoured him much. And he fell in love with the wife of the Count, in the form of pleasure (*a forma de solatz*), and she with him. (The Palma of Browning's poem and the Cunizza of Dante's.) And it befell that the Count stood ill with her brothers. And thus he estranged himself from her and from Sier Sceillme and Sier Albrics. Thus her brothers caused her to be stolen from the Count by Sier Sordello and the latter came to stop with them. And he (Sordello) stayed a long time with them in great happiness, and then he went into Proenssa where he received great honours from all the good men and from the Count and from the Countess who gave him a good castle and a wife of gentle birth." (Browning with perfect right alters this ending to suit his own purpose.)

The luck of the troubadours was as different as their ranks, and they were drawn from all social orders. We are led far from polite and polished society when we come to take note of that Gringoire, Guillem Figiera, "son of a tailor; and he was a tailor; and when the French got hold of Toulouse he departed into Lombardy. And he knew well *trobar* and to sing, and he made himself *joglar* among the townsfolk (*ciutadins*). He was not a man who knew how to carry himself among the barons or among the better class, but much he got himself welcomed among harlots and slatterns and by innkeepers and taverners. And if he saw coming a good man of the court, there where he was, he was sorry and grieved at it, and he nearly split himself to take him down a peg (*et ades percussava de lui abaissar*)."

For one razo that shows an unusual character there are a dozen that say simply that such or such a man was of Manes, or of Cataloigna by Rossilon, or of elsewhere, "a poor cavalier."[1] They made their way by favour at times, or by singing, or by some form of utility. Ademar of Gauvedan "was of the castle Marvois, son of a poor knight. He was knighted by the lord of Marvois. He was a brave man but could not keep his estate as knight, and he became jongleur and was respected by all the best people. And later he went into orders at Gran Mon." Elias Cairels "was of Sarlat; ill he sang, ill he composed, ill he played the fiddle and worse he spoke, but he was good at writing out words and tunes. And he was a long time wandering, and when he quitted it, he returned to Sarlat and died there." Perdigo was the son of a fisherman and made his fortune by his art. Peirol was a poor knight who was fitted out by the Dalfin of Auvergne and made love to Sail de Claustra; and all we know of Cercamon is that he made *vers* and *pastorelas* in the old way and

---

[1] For example Piere Bermon and Palazol.

that "he went everywhere he could get to." Pistoleta "was a singer for Arnaut of Marvoil, and later he took to *trobar* and made songs with pleasing tunes and he was well received by the best people, although a man of little comfort and of poor endowment and of little stamina. And he took a wife at Marseilles and became a merchant and became rich and ceased going about the courts." Guillems the skinny was a joglar of Manes and the capital letter shows him throwing 3, 5, and 4, on a red dice board. "Never had he on harness, and what he gained he lost *malamen*, to the taverns and the women. And he ended in a hospital in Spain."

The razos have in them the seeds of literary criticism. The speech is, however, laconic. Aimar lo Ners was a gentleman. "He made such songs as he knew how to." Aimeric de Sarlat, a joglar, became a troubadour, "and yet he made but one song." Piere Guillem of Toulouse "Made good coblas, but he made too many." Daude of Pradas made canzos "per sen de trobar," which I think we may translate "from a mental grasp of the craft." "But they did not move from love, wherefore they had not favour among folk. They were not sung." We find also that the labour and skill were divided. One man played the viol most excellently, and another sang, and another spoke his songs to music,[1] and another, Jaufre Rudel, Brebezieu's father-in-law, made "good tunes with poor words to go with them."

The troubadour's person comes in for as much free criticism as his performance. Elias fons Slada was a "fair man verily, as to feature, a joglar, no good troubadour."[2] But Faidit, a joglar of Uzerche, "was exceedingly greedy both to drink and to eat, and he became fat beyond measure. And he took to wife a public woman; very fair and well taught she was, but she became as big and fat as he was. And she was from a rich town Alest of the Mark of Provença from the seignory of En Bernart d'Andussa."

One of the noblest figures of the time, if we are to believe the chronicle, was Savaric de Mauleon, the rich baron of Peiteu, mentioned above, son of Sir Reios de Malleon; "lord was he of Malleon and of Talarnom and of Fontenai, and of castle Aillon and of Boetand of Benaon and of St Miquel en Letz and of the isles of Ners and of the isle of Mues and of Nestrine and of Engollius and of many other good places." As one may read in the continuation of this notice and verify from the razos of the other troubadours, "he was of the most open-handed men in the world." He seems to have left little verse save the tenzon with Faidit.

"Behold divers estate between them all!" Yet, despite the difference in conditions of life between the twelfth century and our own, these few citations should be enough to prove that the people were much the same, and if the preceding notes do not do this, there is one tale left that should succeed.

[1] Richard of Brebezieu (disia sons).
[2] The "joglar" was the player and singer, the "troubadour" the "finder" or composer of songs and words.

"The Vicomte of St Antoni was of the bishopric of Caortz (Cahors), Lord and Vicomte of St Antoni; and he loved a noble lady who was wife of the seignor of Pena Dalbeges, of a rich castle and a strong. The lady was gentle and fair and valiant and highly prized and much honoured; and he very valiant and well trained and good at arms and charming, and a good trobaire, and had name Raimons Jordans; and the lady was called the Vicomtesse de Pena; and the love of these two was beyond all measure. And it befell that the Vicount went into a land of his enemies and was grievous wounded, so that report held him for dead. And at the news she in great grief went and gave candles at church for his recovery. And he recovered. And at this news also she had great grief." And she fell a-moping, and that was the end of the affair with St Antoni, and "thus was there more than one in deep distress." "Wherefore" Elis of Montfort, wife of William à-Gordon, daughter of the Viscount of Trozena, the glass of fashion and the mould of form, the pride of "youth, beauty, courtesy," and presumably of justice, mercy, long-suffering, and so forth, made him overtures, and successfully. And the rest is a matter much as usual.

If humanity was much the same, it is equally certain that individuals were not any more like one another; and this may be better shown in the uncommunicative *canzoni* than in the razos. Thus we have a pastoral from the sensitive and little known Joios of Tolosa:

> Lautrier el dous temps de pascor
> En una ribeira,

which runs thus:

"The other day, in the sweet time of Easter, I went across a flat land of rivers hunting for new flowers, walking by the side of the path, and for delight in the greenness of things and because of the complete good faith and love which I bear for her who inspires me, I felt a melting about my heart and at the first flower I found, I burst into tears.

"And I wept until, in a shady place, my eyes fell upon a shepherdess. Fresh was her colour, and she was white as a snow-drift, and she had doves' eyes," . . .

In very different key we find the sardonic Count of Foix, in a song which begins mildly enough for a spring song:

> Mas qui a flor si vol mesclar,

and turns swiftly enough to a livelier measure:

> Ben deu gardar lo sieu baston
> Car frances sabon grans colps dar
> Et albirar ab lor bordon
> E nous fizes in carcasses
> Ni en genes ni en gascon.

Let no man lounge amid the flowers
Without a stout club of some kind.
Know ye the French are stiff in stour
And sing not all they have in mind,
So trust ye not in Carcason,
In Genovese, nor in Gascon.

My purpose in all this is to suggest to the casual reader that the Middle Ages did not exist in the tapestry alone, nor in the fourteenth-century romances, but that there was a life like our own, no mere sequence of citherns and citoles, nor a continuous stalking about in sendal and diaspre. Men were pressed for money. There was unspeakable boredom in the castles. The chivalric singing was devised to lighten the boredom; and this very singing became itself in due time, in the manner of all things, an ennui.

There has been so much written about the poetry of the best Provençal period, to wit the end of the twelfth century, that I shall say nothing of it here, but shall confine the latter part of this essay to a mention of three efforts, or three sorts of effort which were made to keep poetry alive after the crusade of 1208.

Any study of European poetry is unsound if it does not commence with a study of that art in Provence. The art of quantitative verse had been lost. This loss was due more to ignorance than to actual changes of language, from Latin, that is, into the younger tongues. It is open to doubt whether the Aeolic singing was ever comprehended fully even in Rome. When men began to write on tablets and ceased singing to the *barbitos*, a loss of some sort was unavoidable. Propertius may be cited as an exception, but Propertius writes only one meter. In any case the classic culture of the Renaissance was grafted on to medieval culture, a process which is excellently illustrated by Andreas Divus Iustinopolitanus's translation of the *Odyssey* into Latin. It is true that each century after the Renaissance has tried in its own way to come nearer the classic, but, if we are to understand that part of our civilization which is the art of verse, we must begin at the root, and that root is medieval. The poetic art of Provence paved the way for the poetic art of Tuscany; and to this Dante bears sufficient witness in the *De Vulgari Eloquio*. The heritage of art is one thing to the public and quite another to the succeeding artists. The artist's inheritance from other artists can be little more than certain enthusiasms, which usually spoil his first work; and a definite knowledge of the modes of expression, which knowledge contributes to perfecting his more mature performance. This is a matter of technique.

After the compositions of Vidal, Rudel, Ventadour, of Bornelh and Bertrans de Born and Arnaut Daniel, there seemed little chance of doing distinctive work in the "canzon de l'amour courtois." There was no way, or at least there was no man in Provence capable of finding a new way of saying in six closely rhymed strophes that a certain girl, matron or widow was like a certain set of things, and that the troubadour's virtues were like another set, and that all this was very sorrowful or otherwise, and that there was but one obvious remedy. Richard of Brebezieu had done his best for tired ears; he had made similes of beasts and of stars which got him a passing favour. He had compared himself to the fallen elephant and to the self-piercing pelican, and no one could go any further. Novelty is reasonably rare even in modes of decadence and revival. The three devices tried for poetic restoration in the early thirteenth century were the three usual devices. Certain men turned to talking art and aesthetics and attempted to dress up the folk-song. Certain men tried to make verse more engaging by stuffing it with an intellectual and argumentative content. Certain men turned to social satire. Roughly, we may divide the interesting work of the later Provençal period into these three divisions. As all of these men had progeny in Tuscany, they are, from the historical point of view, worth a few moments' attention.

The first school is best represented in the work of Giraut Riquier of Narbonne. His most notable feat was the revival of the *Pastorela*. The Pastorela is a poem in which a knight tells of having met with a shepherdess or some woman of that class, and of what fortune and conversation befell him. The form had been used long before by Marcabrun, and is familiar to us in such poems as Guido Cavalcanti's *In un boschetto trovai pastorella*, or in Swinburne's *An Interlude*. Guido, who did all things well, whenever the fancy took him, has raised this form to a surpassing excellence in his poem *Era in pensier d'Amor, quand' io trovai*. Riquier is most amusing in his account of the inn-mistress at Sant Pos de Tomeiras, but even there he is less amusing than was Marcabrun when he sang of the shepherdess in *L'autrier iost' una sebissa*. Riquier has, however, his place in the apostolic succession; and there is no reason why Cavalcanti and Riquier should not have met while the former was on his journey to Campostella, although Riquier may as easily have not been in Spain at the time. At any rate the Florentine noble would have heard the *Pastorelas* of Giraut; and this may have set him to his *ballate*, which seem to date from the time of his meeting with Mandetta in Toulouse. Or it may have done nothing of the kind. The only more or less settled fact is that Riquier was then the best known living troubadour and near the end of his course.

The second, and to us the dullest of the schools, set to explaining the nature of love and its effects. The normal modern will probably slake all his curiosity for this sort of work in reading one such poem as the King of Navarre's *De Fine amour vient science e beautez*. "Ingenium nobis ipsa puella fecit," as Propertius put it, or *anglice:*

> Knowledge and beauty from true love are wrought,
> And likewise love is born from this same pair;
> These three are one to whomso hath true thought, etc.

There might be less strain if one sang it. This peculiar variety of flame was carried to the altars of Bologna, whence Guinicello sang:

> Al cor gentil ripara sempre amore,
> Come l'augello in selva alla verdura

And Cavalcanti wrote: "A lady asks me, wherefore I wish to speak of an accident[1] which is often cruel," and Dante, following in his elders' footsteps, the *Convito*.

The third school is the school of satire, and is the only one which gives us a contact with the normal life of the time. There had been Provençal satire before Piere Cardinal; but the sirventes of Sordello and De Born were directed for the most part againt persons, while the Canon of Clermont drives rather against conditions. In so far as Dante is critic of morals, Cardinal must be held as his forerunner. Miquel writes of him as follows:

"Piere Cardinal was of Veillac of the city Pui Ma Donna, and he was of honourable lineage, son of a knight and a lady. And when he was little his father put him for canon in the *canonica major* of Puy; and he learnt letters, and he knew well how to read and to sing; and when he was come to man's estate he had high knowledge of the vanity of this world, for he felt himself gay and fair and young. And he made many fair arguments and fair songs. And he made canzos, but he made only a few of these, and sirventes; and he did best in the said sirventes where he set forth many fine arguments and fair examples for those who understand them; for much he rebuked the folly of this world and much he reproved the false clerks, as his sirventes show. And he went through the courts of kings and of noble barons and took with him his joglar who sang the sirventes. And much was he honoured and welcomed by my lord the good king of Aragon and by honourable barons. And I, master Miquel de la Tour, escriuan (scribe), do ye to wit that N. Piere Cardinal when he passed from this life was nearly a hundred. And I, the aforesaid Miquel, have written these sirventes in the city of Nemze (Nîmes) and here are written some of his sirventes."

If the Vicomtesse de Pena reminds us of certain ladies whom we have met, these sirventes of Cardinal may well remind us that thoughtful men have in every age found almost the same set of things or at least the same sort of things to protest against; if it be not a corrupt press or some monopoly, it is always some sort of equivalent, some conspiracy of ignorance and interest. And thus he says, "Li clerc si fan pastor." The clerks pretend to be shepherds, but they are wolfish at heart.

If he can find a straight man, it is truly matter for song; and so we hear him say of the Duke of Narbonne, who was apparently, making a fight for honest administration:

---

[1] *Accidente*, used as a purely technical term of his scholastic philosophy.

> Coms raymon duc de Narbona
> Marques de proensa
> Vostra valors es tan bona
> Que tot lo mon gensa,
> Quar de la mar de bayona
> En tro a valenca
> Agra gent falsae fellona
> Lai ab vil temensa,
> Mas vos tenetz vil lor
> Q'n frances bevedor
> Plus qua perditz austor
> No vos fan temensa.

"Now is come from France what one did not ask for"—he is addressing the man who is standing against the North—

> Count Raymon, Duke of Narbonne,
> Marquis of Provence,
> Your valour is sound enough
> To make up for the cowardice of
> All the rest of the gentry.
> For from the sea at Bayonne,
> Even to Valence,
> Folk would have given in (sold out),
> But you hold them in scorn,
> [Or, reading "l'aur," "scorn the gold."]
> So that the drunken French
> Alarm you no more
> Than a partridge frightens a hawk.

Cardinal is not content to spend himself in mere abuse, like the little tailor Figeira, who rhymes Christ's "mortal pena" with

> Car voletz totzjors portar la borsa plena,

which is one way of saying "Judas!" to the priests. He, Cardinal, sees that the technique of honesty is not always utterly simple.

> Li postilh, legat elh cardinal
> La cordon tug, y an fag establir
> Que qui nos pot de traisson esdir,

which may mean, "The pope and the legate and the cardinal have twisted such a cord that they have brought things to such a pass that no one can escape committing treachery." As for the rich:

> Li ric home an pietat tan gran
> Del autre gen quon ac caym da bel.

Que mais volon tolre q̄ lop no fan
E mais mentir que tozas de bordelh.

The rich men have such pity
For other folk—about as much as Cain had for Abel.
For they would like to leave less than the wolves do,
And to lie more than girls in a brothel.

Of the clergy, "A tantas vey baylia," "So much the more do I see clerks
coming into power that all the world will be theirs, whoever objects. For
they'll have it with taking or with giving" (i.e. by granting land, belonging to
one man, to someone else who will pay allegiance for it, as in the case of De
Montfort), "or with pardon or with hypocrisy; or by assault or by drinking
and eating; or by prayers or by praising the worse; or with God or with
devilry." We find him putting the age-long query about profit in the following:

He may have enough harness
And sorrel horses and bays;
Tower, wall, and palace,
May he have
—the rich man denying his God.

The stanza runs very smoothly to the end.

Si mortz no fos
Elh valgra per un cen

A hundred men he would be worth
Were there no death.

The modern Provençal enthusiast in raptures at the idea of chivalric love (a
term which he usually misunderstands), and little concerned with the art of
verse, has often failed to notice how finely the sound of Cardinal's poems is
matched with their meaning. There is a lash and sting in his timbre and in his
movement. Yet the old man is not always bitter; or, if he is bitter, it is with
the bitterness of a torn heart and not a hard one. It is so we find him in the
sirvente beginning:

As a man weeps for his son or for his father,
Or for his friend when death has taken him,
So do I mourn for the living who do their own ill,
False, disloyal, felon, and full of ill-fare,
Deceitful, breakers-of-pact,
Cowards, complainers,
Highwaymen, thieves-by-stealth, turn-coats,
Betrayers, and full of treachery,

> Here where the devil reigns
>   And teaches them to act thus.

He is almost the only singer of his time to protest against the follies of war. As here:

> Ready for war, as night is to follow the sun,
> Readier for it than is the fool to be cuckold
> When he has first plagued his wife!
> And war is an ill thing to look upon,
> And I know that there is not one man drawn into it
> But his child, or his cousin or someone akin to him
> Prays God that it be given over.

He says plainly, in another place, that the barons make war for their own profit, regardless of the peasants. "Fai mal senher vas los sieu." His sobriety is not to be fooled with sentiment either martial or otherwise. There is in him little of the fashion of feminolatry, and the gentle reader in search of trunk-hose and the light guitar had better go elsewhere. As for women: "L'una fai drut."

> One turns leman for the sake of great possessions;
> And another because poverty is killing her,
> And one hasn't even a shift of coarse linen;
> And another has two and does likewise.
> And one gets an old man—and she is a young wench,
> And the old woman gives the man an elixir.

As for justice, there is little now: "If a rich man steal by chicanery, he will have right before Constantine (i.e. by legal circumambience) but the poor thief may go hang." And after this there is a passage of pity and of irony fine-drawn as much of his work is, for he keeps the very formula that De Born had used in his praise of battle, "Belh mes quan vey"; and, perhaps, in Sir Bertrans' time even the Provençal wars may have seemed more like a game, and may have appeared to have some element of sport and chance in them. But the twelfth century had gone, and the spirit of the people was weary, and the old canon's passage may well serve as a final epitaph on all that remained of silk thread and *cisclatons*, of viol and *gai saber*.

> Never agin shall we see the Easter come in so fairly,
> That was wont to come in with pleasure and with song,
> No! but we see it arrayed with alarms and excursions,
> Arrayed with war and dismay and fear,
> Arrayed with troops and with cavalcades,
> Oh, yes, it's a fine sight to see holder and shepherd
> Going so wretched that they know not where they are

APPENDIX 2

The Gypsy

"Est-ce que vous avez vu des autres—des camarades—avec des singes ou des ours?"
A Stray Gipsy—A.D. 1912

That was the top of the walk, when he said:
"Have you seen any others, any of our lot,
With apes or bears?"
          —A brown upstanding fellow
Not like the half-castes,
           up on the wet road near Clermont.
The wind came, and the rain,
And mist clotted about the trees in the valley,
And I'd the long ways behind me,
          gray Arles and Biaucaire,
And he said, "Have you seen any of our lot?"
I'd seen a lot of his lot . . .
          ever since Rhodez,
Coming down from the fair
         of St. John,
With caravans, but never an ape or a bear.

Provincia Deserta

At Rochecoart,
Where the hills part
         in three ways,
And three valleys, full of winding roads,
Fork out to south and north,
There is a place of trees . . . gray with lichen.
I have walked there
         thinking of old days.
At Chalais
         is a pleached arbour;
Old pensioners and old protected women
Have the right there—

it is charity.
I have crept over old rafters,
              peering down
Over the Dronne,
              over a stream full of lilies.
Eastward the road lies,
              Aubeterre is eastward,
With a garrulous old man at the inn.
I know the roads in that place:
Mareuil to the north-east,
              La Tour,
There are three keeps near Mareuil,
And an old woman,
              glad to hear Arnaut,
Glad to lend one dry clothing.

I have walked
              into Perigord,
I have seen the torch-flames, high-leaping,
Painting the front of that church;
Heard, under the dark, whirling laughter.
I have looked back over the stream
              and seen the high building,
Seen the long minarets, the white shafts.
I have gone in Ribeyrac
              and in Sarlat,
I have climbed rickety stairs, heard talk of Croy,
Walked over En Bertran's old layout,
Have seen Narbonne, and Cahors and Chalus,
Have seen Excideuil, carefully fashioned.

I have said:
              "Here such a one walked.
Here Cœur-de-Lion was slain.
              Here was good singing.
Here one man hastened his step.
              Here one lay panting."
I have looked south from Hautefort,
              thinking of Montaignac, southward.
I have lain in Rocafixada,
              level with sunset,
Have seen the copper come down
              tingeing the mountains,
I have seen the fields, pale, clear as an emerald,

Sharp peaks, high spurs, distant castles.
I have said: "The old roads have lain here.
Men have gone by such and such valleys
Where the great halls were closer together."
I have seen Foix on its rock, seen Toulouse, and
                    Arles greatly altered,
I have seen the ruined "Dorata."
                    I have said:
"Riquier! Guido."
                    I have thought of the second Troy,
Some little prized place in Auvergnat:
Two men tossing a coin, one keeping a castle,
One set on the highway to sing.
                    He sang a woman.
Auvergne rose to the song;
                    The Dauphin backed him.
"The castle to Austors!"
                    "Pieire kept the singing—
A fair man and a pleasant."
                    He won the lady,
Stole her away for himself, kept her against armed
                    force:
So ends that story.
That age is gone;
Pieire de Maensac is gone.
I have walked over these roads;
I have thought of them living.

Near Perigord

> *A Perigord, pres del muralh*
> *Tan que i puosch' om gitar ab malh.*

You'd have men's hearts up from the dust
And tell their secrets, Messire Cino,
Right enough? Then read between the lines of Uc St. Circ,
Solve me the riddle, for you know the tale.

Bertrans, En Bertrans, left a fine canzone:
"Maent, I love you, you have turned me out.
The voice at Montfort, Lady Agnes' hair,
Bel Miral's stature, the viscountess' throat,

Set all together, are not worthy of you. . . ."
And all the while you sing out that canzone,
Think you that Maent lived at Montagnac,
One at Chalais, another at Malemort
Hard over Brive—for every lady a castle,
Each place strong.

      Oh, *is* it easy enough?
Tairiran held hall in Montagnac,
His brother-in-law was all there was of power
In Perigord, and this good union
Gobbled all the land, and held it later for some hundred years.
And our En Bertrans was in Altafort,
Hub of the wheel, the stirrer-up of strife,
As caught by Dante in the last wallow of hell—
The headless trunk "that made its head a lamp,"
For separation wrought out separation,
And he who set the strife between brother and brother
And had his way with the old English king,
Viced in such torture for the "counterpass."

How would you live, with neighbours set about you—
Poictiers and Brive, untaken Rochecouart,
Spread like the finger-tips of one frail hand;
And you on that great mountain of a palm—
Not a neat ledge, not Foix between its streams,
But one huge back half-covered up with pine,
Worked for and snatched from the string-purse of Born—
The four round towers, four brothers—mostly fools:
What could he do but play the desperate chess,
And stir old grudges?
      "Pawn your castles, lords!
Let the Jews pay."
      And the great scene—
(That, maybe, never happened!)
      Beaten at last,
Before the hard old king:
      "Your son, ah, since he died
My wit and worth are cobwebs brushed aside
In the full flare of grief. Do what you will."

Take the whole man, and ravel out the story.
He loved this lady in castle Montagnac?

The castle flanked him—he had need of it.
You read to-day, how long the overlords of Perigord,
The Talleyrands, have held the place; it was no transient fiction.
And Maent failed him? Or saw through the scheme?

And all his net-like thought of new alliance?
Chalais is high, a-level with the poplars.
Its lowest stones just meet the valley tips
Where the low Dronne is filled with water-lilies.
And Rochecouart can match it, stronger yet,
The very spur's end, built on sheerest cliff,
And Malemort keeps its close hold on Brive,
While Born, his own close purse, his rabbit warren,
His subterranean chamber with a dozen doors,
A-bristle with antennæ to feel roads,
To sniff the traffic into Perigord.
And that hard phalanx, that unbroken line,
The ten good miles from there to Maent's castle,
All of his flank—how could he do without her?
And all the road to Cahors, to Toulouse?
What would he do without her?

"Papiol,
Go forthright singing—Anhes, Cembelins.
There is a throat; ah, there are two white hands;
There is a trellis full of early roses,
And all my heart is bound about with love.
Where am I come with compound flatteries—
What doors are open to fine compliment?"
And every one half jealous of Maent?
He wrote the catch to pit their jealousies
Against her; give her pride in them?

Take his own speech, make what you will of it—
And still the knot, the first knot, of Maent?

Is it a love poem? Did he sing of war?
Is it an intrigue to run subtly out,
Born of a jongleur's tongue, freely to pass
Up and about and in and out the land,
Mark him a craftsman and a strategist?
(St. Leider had done as much at Polhonac,
Singing a different stave, as closely hidden.)

Oh, there is precedent, legal tradition,
To sing one thing when your song means another,
"*Et albirar ab lor bordon*—"
Foix' count knew that. What is Sir Bertrans' singing?

Maent, Maent, and yet again Maent,
Or war and broken heaumes and politics?

II

End fact. Try fiction. Let us say we see
En Bertrans, a tower-room at Hautefort,
Sunset, the ribbon-like road lies, in red cross-light,
Southward toward Montagnac, and he bends at a table
Scribbling, swearing between his teeth; by his left hand
Lie little strips of parchment covered over,
Scratched and erased with *al* and *ochaisos*.
Testing his list of rhymes, a lean man? Bilious?
With a red straggling beard?
And the green cat's-eye lifts toward Montagnac.

Or take his "magnet" singer setting out,
Dodging his way past Aubeterre, singing at Chalais
In the vaulted hall,
Or, by a lichened tree at Rochecouart
Aimlessly watching a hawk above the valleys,
Waiting his turn in the mid-summer evening,
Thinking of Aelis, whom he loved heart and soul . . .
To find her half alone, Montfort away,
And a brown, placid, hated woman visiting her,
Spoiling his visit, with a year before the next one.
Little enough?
Or carry him forward. "Go through all the courts,
My Magnet," Bertrans had said.

We came to Ventadour
In the mid love court, he sings out the canzon,
No one hears save Arrimon Luc D'Esparo—
No one hears aught save the gracious sound of compliments.
Sir Arrimon counts on his fingers, Montfort,
Rochecouart, Chalais, the rest, the tactic,
Malemort, guesses beneath, sends word to Cœur-de-Lion:

The compact, de Born smoked out, trees felled
About his castle, cattle driven out!
Or no one sees it, and En Bertrans prospered?

    And ten years after, or twenty, as you will,
Arnaut and Richard lodge beneath Chalus:
The dull round towers encroaching on the field,
The tents tight drawn, horses at tether
Further and out of reach, the purple night,
The crackling of small fires, the bannerets,
The lazy leopards on the largest banner,
Stray gleams on hanging mail, an armourer's torch-flare
Melting on steel.

    And in the quietest space
They probe old scandals, say de Born is dead;
And we've the gossip (skipped six hundred years).
Richard shall die to-morrow—leave him there
Talking of *trobar clus* with Daniel.
And the "best craftsman" sings out his friend's song,
Envies it vigour . . . and deplores the technique,
Dispraises his own skill?—That's as you will.
And they discuss the dead man,
Plantagenet puts the riddle: "Did he love her?"
And Arnaut parries: "Did he love your sister?
True, he has praised her, but in some opinion
He wrote that praise only to show he had
The favour of your party; had been well received."

"You knew the man."
        "*You* knew the man.
I am an artist, you have tried both métiers."
"You were born near him."
        "Do we know our friends?"
"Say that he saw the castles, say that he loved Maent!"
"Say that he loved her, does it solve the riddle?"
  End the discussion, Richard goes out next day
And gets a quarrel-bolt shot through his vizard,
Pardons the bowman, dies,

    Ends our discussion. Arnaut ends
"In sacred odour"—(that's apocryphal!)
And we can leave the talk till Dante writes:

Surely I saw, and still before my eyes
Goes on that headless trunk, that bears for light
Its own head swinging, gripped by the dead hair,
And like a swinging lamp that says, "Ah me!
I severerd men, my head and heart
Ye see here severed, my life's counterpart."

Or take En Bertrans?

III

Ed eran due in uno, ed uno in due;
Inferno, XXVIII, 125

Bewildering spring, and by the Auvezere
Poppies and day's eyes in the green émail
Rose over us; and we knew all that stream,
And our two horses had traced out the valleys;
Knew the low flooded lands squared out with poplars,
In the young days when the deep sky befriended.
　　　And great wings beat above us in the twilight,
And the great wheels in heaven
Bore us together . . . surging . . . and apart . . .
Believing we should meet with lips and hands,

　High, high and sure . . . and then the counter-thrust:
'Why do you love me? Will you always love me?
But I am like the grass, I can not love you.'
Or, 'Love, and I love and love you,
And hate your mind, not *you*, your soul, your hands.'

　So to this last estrangement, Tairiran!

　There shut up in his castle, Tairiran's,
She who had nor ears nor tongue save in her hands,
Gone—ah, gone—untouched, unreachable!
She who could never live save through one person,
She who could never speak save to one person,
And all the rest of her a shifting change,
A broken bundle of mirrors . . . !

Notes to Introduction

1. Donald Davie, *"The Cantos:* Towards a Pedestrian Reading," *Paideuma*, vol. 1, no. 1 (Spring 1972), pp. 55–62. Davie's initial explorations of the countryside around Chalais and Aubeterre pointed the way to this edition of the *Walking Tour*.

2. The standard monographs on Pound and Provençal poetry are Stuart Y. Mc-Dougal, *Ezra Pound and the Troubadour Tradition* (Princeton, 1972) and Peter Makin, *Provence and Pound* (Berkeley, 1978). Pound's early academic career is examined in J. J. Wilhelm, *The American Roots of Ezra Pound* (New York, 1985).

3. The Seymour Company of Chicago (publishers of *Poetry* magazine) advertised Pound's Arnaut Daniel edition as forthcoming in 1913 but subsequently decided against publication. In 1918, Pound sent a revised version of the book off to a Cleveland publisher, but the manuscript never reached its destination (with Pound concluding it had either been censored or "submarined"). See Donald Gallup, *Ezra Pound: A Bibliography* (Charlottesville, 1983), p. 446.

4. R. Murray Schafer, *Ezra Pound and Music: The Complete Criticism* (New York, 1977), pp. 7–12.

5. Rummel's collection of songs included the two Arnaut melodies Pound had dug up at the Ambrosian library. Pound also later collaborated with Agnes Bedford on *Five Troubadour Songs* (London, 1920). Rummel's 1913 setting of "Mère au Sauveur" in *Hesternae Rosae* was later used by Pound in his 1926 opera *Le Testament*. Schafer, pp. 27–28, and Gallup, p. 438.

6. Hugh Kenner's analysis of Arnaut's craft of *motz el son* remains unsurpassed; see *The Pound Era* (Berkeley, 1971), pp. 76–93, 111–20, 368–77.

7. Justin Smith, *The Troubadours at Home: Their Lives and Personalities. Their Songs and Their World*, 2 vols. (New York, 1899). Pound was also familiar with Ida Farnell's popular *Lives of the Troubadours: Translated from the Original Provençal* (London, 1896). See Makin, p. 284.

8. Makin, p. 62, and William D. Paden Jr., "Pound's Use of Troubadour Manuscripts," *Comparative Literature*, vol. 32, no. 4 (Fall 1980), pp. 402–11.

9. See Omar Pound and Robert Spoo, eds., *Ezra Pound and Margaret Cravens: A Tragic Friendship 1910–1912* (Durham, 1988). Walter Morse Rummel introduced Margaret Cravens to Pound while the latter was passing through Paris in March 1911 en route to Italy. On the basis of this brief acquaintance, the American heiress (and descendant of Sidney Lanier) contributed roughly $1,000 per year to Pound's upkeep (the equivalent of about $10,000 today). The romantic friendship between the two deepened over the course of Pound's stay in Paris the following spring—Cravens was the "Weaver of Beauty" to whom Rummel's 1911 settings of *Three Songs of Ezra Pound* were dedicated. Further complicating the triangle that existed between himself, Rummel, and Cravens, Pound induced his patroness to host his ex-fiancées Mary Moore and Hilda Doolittle during their visits to Paris. Over the course of his stay at Rummel's Passy flat in the spring of 1912, Pound continued to cultivate Cravens's *amitié*

amoureuse: on May 26, on the eve of his departure for the Midi, he visited her at home to celebrate her thirty-first birthday. Six days later, on June 1st, she put a pistol to her right breast. Omar Pound and Robert Spoo mention evidence that her suicide might have been precipitated by a letter or telegram that Pound had sent from the South of France (possibly announcing he would not marry her), but they conclude that the more likely cause of her death was her discovery that Rummel had betrayed her by becoming secretly engaged to her friend Thérèse Chaigneau.

10. Omar Pound and A. Walton Litz, eds., *Ezra Pound and Dorothy Shakespear: Their Letters 1909–1914* (New York, 1984), p. 122.

11. Letter to Frances Weston, Oct. 1912, at the Beinecke Library, Yale University.

12. *Ezra Pound and Dorothy Shakespear*, pp. 150, 155, 158, 161.

13. Ibid., pp. 122 and 162.

14. Letter to Alice Corbin Henderson, at the Humanities Research Center, University of Texas at Austin.

15. The lines occur at the outset of Ur-Canto 1 (1917). On ghosts and genies of place see Geoffrey H. Hartman, "Romantic Poetry and the Genius Loci," in *Beyond Formalism* (New Haven, 1970), pp. 311–36.

16. Tony Tanner, "American and European Romanticism," in *Scenes of Nature, Signs of Men* (Cambridge, 1987), pp. 25–45.

17. First published in *Umbra* (1920), but identified in the table of contents as composed in 1912. For a further examination of Pound's hieratic morphologies of landscape, see John Peck's brilliant reading of "Landscape as Ceremony in the later Cantos," *Agenda*, vol. 9, nos. 2–3 (1971), pp. 26–69.

18. Reproduced as "Fragment 4B" of Canto 4 in Christine Froula, *To Write Paradise: Style and Error in Pound's Cantos* (New Haven, 1984), p. 104.

19. The phrase occurs in Ur-Canto 1: the full text of these "Three Cantos" (1917) may be found at the end of the new revised edition of *Personae* prepared by Lea Baechler and A. Walton Litz (New York, 1990). For a detailed account of the origins of Pound's long poem, see Ronald Bush, *The Genesis of Ezra Pound's Cantos* (Princeton, 1976). Behind the problematic precursor figure of Browning in these Ur-Cantos lies "that bleating sheep, Will Wordsworth" whose influence Pound still seems anxiously trying to repress.

20. Cited and glossed in Kevin Oderman, *Ezra Pound and the Erotic Medium* (Durham, 1986), pp. 43ff.

21. See Hugh Kenner's magisterial reading of this Arnaut Canto in *The Pound Era*, pp. 112–20.

Notes to a Walking Tour

POITIERS AND ANGOULÊME

1. The Romanesque cathedral of Notre-Dame-La Grande, built toward the end of the 11th century, is especially noted for its elaborate west façade, which is described by the 1907 Baedeker as being "flanked by turrets with conical tops and fish-scale ornamentation." The same terms recur in Canto 4 to evoke the Ovidian Languedoc landscape associated with Peire Vidal/Actaeon: "The sunlight glitters, glitters a-top, / Like a fish-scale roof, / Like the church roof in Poictiers / If it were gold" (4/14).

2. A reference to the discussion of the realist "prose tradition" of Flaubert, Maupassant, and the Goncourts in Ford Maddox Hueffer's *The Critical Attitude* (1911).

3. St. Peter's cathedral was begun in 1162 by Henry II (1133–83), husband of Eleanor of Aquitaine (1122?–1204) and father of Richard I, Coeur de Lion (1157–99)—all of whom figure in Canto 6, a collage of historical documents that traces the turbulent lineage of troubadour culture over two centuries from Poitiers to the Italy of Sordello. *Si fos de Limousi* ("He was of Limousin") was a standard opening phrase in many troubadour *vidas* or biographies.

4. Judging from its idiosyncratic Provençal, this *canso* seems to be of Pound's own invention (he refers to it slightly later on as "my canzon"). Rough translation: "As the flower / which entwines / and blooms, fragrant / And is not harmed or deceived / By the bits of crossed wood." In Ur-Canto 2 (published in *Poetry* in 1917), Pound quotes the same poem, this time attributing it to the troubadour Raimons Jordans, Viscount of St. Antoni: "Viscount of St. Antoni / In the warm damp of spring, / Feeling the night air full of subtle hands, / Plucks at a viol, singing: / "As the rose— / Si com, si com"—they all being *"si com."* / "For as the rose in trellis / Winds in and through and over, / So is your beauty in my heart, that is bound through and over. / So lay Queen Venus in her house of glass, / The pool of worth thou art, / Flood-land of pleasure."

5. A game played with marbles ("pigs") on a small rimmed and often glass-covered board, which is tilted to get each marble into a designated hole.

6. The church of St. Radegonde was established as a shrine around 560 and rebuilt in the 11th-13th centuries.

7. François Mansart or Mansard, the 17th-century architect whose name is associated with the steeply pitched roof characteristic of much French urban architecture.

8. An "enclosed" or hermetic troubadour composition containing hidden or esoteric meanings.

9. The colossal gilded statue of Notre Dame des Dunes dominates the river Clain on the outskirts of Poitiers.

10. Parish church?

11. Clear, crisp weather, as in the Viscount of St Antoni's "Lo clar temps vei brunezir" (LE, 114).

12. Situated on an eminence between the Charente and Anguienne rivers. Angoulême is approached by elevated rail through the faubourg de l'Houmeau to the northeast, with a view on the steeple of St. Martial and the tower of the Hôtel de Ville.

III

13. The 12th-century cathedral of St. Peter, whose Romanesque architecture resembles that of Notre-Dame in Poitiers and St. Front in Périgueux.

14. Pound's series of essays on America, "Patria Mia" (1912), exuberantly praise the skyscrapers of New York: "Squares after squares of flame, set and cut into the ether. Here is our poetry, for we have pulled down the stars to our will" (SP, 107).

15. Gautier? Gourmont?

16. Cf. Pound's favorite Spinoza tag: "The intellectual love of a thing consists in the understanding of its perfections" (LE, 71).

17. In his *Little Tour in Southern France* (1884), Henry James had lensed his evocation of Angoulême through Balzac's description of the town in *Illusions perdues*. Pound's later comments on James' Balzacian Angoulême corroborate his own 1912 doubts concerning the realist novel's portraiture of place: "The disadvantage of giving impressions of real instead of imaginary places is that they conflict with other people's impressions. I do not see Angoulême via Balzac, nor do I feel Henry James' contacts with the places where our tracks have crossed, very remarkable. I dare say it is a good enough guide for people more meagrely furnished with associations or perceptions. Allow me my *piéton's* shrug for a man who has gone only by train. Henry James is not very deep in ancient associations" (LE, 330).

CHALAIS AND RIBÉRAC

1. The 12th-century Romanesque cathedral of St. Peter lies at the southwestern perimeter of Angoulême.

2. "May was the month, and soft / The singing nights; up aloft / The quarter moon swam and scoffed / His unease . . ." From Maurice Hewlett's "Lai of Gaubertz," first published in the *Fortnightly Review* (1 May 1912) with the acknowledgment, "I owe the substance of this *lai* to my friend Ezra Pound, who unearthed it . . . in some Provençal repertory."

3. Translation: "The Vicountess of Chalais / her throat and her two hands." From Bertran de Born's *"Dompna pois de me no'us chal."* The term "dompna soiseubuda" means "imaginary" or "borrowed" Lady.

4. This passing reference to "a perhaps mistaken cause" may contain the seed for Pound's poem "Near Perigord"—the "cause" perhaps being Bertran de Born's rebellion against Richard Coeur de Lion or his conflicts with the counts of Périgord. Pound's interest in Chalais may also have been whetted by Smith's evocation of the place in *The Troubadours at Home*, where he identifies the vicountess of Chalais as Lady Tiborc and imagines Bertran going to visit her in her castle: "But even this brave compliment was ineffectual; and at length, feeling much like a dog without a master, poor Born crossed the hills, and rode on till the woody meadows of the Teude grew narrow, and the highlands thrust a wedge of rock between the river and its confluent. At the point of the wedge stood Chalais. A comfortable chateau is there now, looking down complacently upon the marshes and the poplars; but in those days a lord whose mother was probably Bernart de Ventadorn's Margarida had a mighty fortress on the cliff, with stout walls and high towers for defence, and under the ground safe passages for retreat. The châtelaine—she of the beautiful neck and hands—was a friend of

Bertran's; and the troubadour, after endeavoring to justify his conduct in breaking with Maeut, begged Lady Tiborc to accept him as her knight" (II, 228).

5. A *razo* is the explanatory note that often accompanies the medieval manuscript transcriptions of troubadour songs. Pound observes in "Troubadours: Their Sorts and Traditions" that "The razos have in them the seeds of literary criticism" (LE, 99). Aubeterre is etymologically rooted in "Albaterre" ("white earth").

6. Possible allusion to Pound's 1911 translation of Arnaut Daniel's "*Chansson do-ill mot son plan e prin*": "I'll make a song   with exquisite/Clear words, for buds are blowing sweet/Where the sprays meet,/And flowers don/Their bold blazon/Where leafage springeth greenly/O'ershadowing/The birds that sing/And cry in coppice seemly." (T, 416)

7. A reference to "*Lo ferm voler qu'el cor m'intra*," Arnaut Daniel's famous "nails and uncles" song (cf. 6/21). The last two lines of its first stanza run: "Sivals a frau, lai on non aurai oncle,/Jauzirai joi, en *vergier* o dinz *cambra*" ["Then by stealth, where I'll have no guardian uncle/I shall take my pleasure, in *bower* or in *bedroom*"].

8. Orchard (*vergier*) and garden (*ort*), as opposed to the open fields (*prada*).

9. Presumably Pound's own composition in the manner of Arnaut Daniel. Cf. the translation "Vergier" in his 1918 medley "Langue d'Oc."

10. Arnaut Daniel was born in Ribérac in a castle overlooking the river Dronne; the troubadour Guilhem de la Tor was a native of the nearby village of La Tour Blanche; *lui de Mareuil* (i.e., "the one from Mareuil") was the troubadour Arnaut de Mareuil.

11. Pound confuses the town of Chapteuil (near Le Puy), the place of origin of the troubadour Pons de Capdeuil (or Capduelh), with the village Chapdeuil near La Tour Blanche.

12. Cf. Smith's description in *The Troubadours at Home:* "Ribérac, a small country town, is a newly made railway terminus, and plumes itself with the airs of certain bustling importance. Warlike, or even grand, there is nothing. Below the town lie the rich meadows of the Dronne, and then comes the river itself with its escort of polars and its operatic washerwomen rinsing clothes in the bright water. The castle where Daniel was born stood on a low hill overlooking the meadows and the town, but nothing remains of it except the church" (II, 291).

MAREUIL AND PERIGUEUX

1. Pound seems to have lost his sense of orientation here; walking northward from Celles, Aubeterre and St. Martial would lie to the west and Chapdeuil to the east.

2. The castle passed into the Talleyrand Périgord family in the early 17th century, and in 1883, the Prince de Talleyrand Périgord donated it to the Hospices of Chalais as a source of farm income.

3. Originally erected in 984–1047, rebuilt in 1125 after a fire, the cathedral of St. Front is Byzantine in design, presenting the form of a Greek cross with cupolas which recall those of San Marco in Venice; it is considered the first church in which the pointed arch was systematically introduced. The edifice was completely restored in the second half of the 19th century by Abadie, the architect of the Sacré-Cœur in Paris.

4. *Pèlerinage Charlemagne* (or "Le Voyage à Jerusalem et Constantinople"), a *chanson de geste* of the early 12th century.

5. Adjoining the cathedral of St. Front on the west, rises a 197-foot tower, dating from the beginning of the 11th century—the oldest in France and said to be the only one extant in the Byzantine style. Pound alludes to it in The Pisan Cantos—"But that New York I have found at Périgueux" (80/522)—implicitly comparing it to New York's Metropolitan Life Tower (SP, 105). The gold of Saint Marco's dome is again evoked in Canto 17/78: "In the gloom the gold / Gathers the light about it."

6. According to Pound's account of the genesis of "In a Station of the Metro," a similar *unanimiste* experience of the crowd in Paris in the spring of 1911 or 1912 lay behind his most celebrated Imagist distich: "The apparition of these faces in the crowd: / Petals on a wet, black bough."

7. The Feast of the Trinity is celebrated on the first Sunday after Pentecost; in 1912, it fell on June 2.

HAUTEFORT

1. Pound noted in the commentary on "Near Perigord" published in *Poetry* in 1915: "As to the possibility of a political intrigue behind the apparent love poem we have no evidence save that offered by my own observation of the geography of Perigord and Limoges." In *Provence and Pound* (Berkeley, 1978), Peter Makin outlines Pound's various factual errors in the poem, concluding that "Near Perigord" should be read as mythopoeia "since it sets out to go beyond the known facts, but it tramples all over these facts in the process" (p. 25). The editors of the most recent scholarly edition of Bertran's poetry also dismiss Pound's attempt to read *"Dompna pois"* as political allegory; see William D. Paden, Jr., Tilde Sankovitch, Patricia Stäblein, eds., *The Poems of the Troubadour Bertran de Born* (Berkeley, 1986), pp. 79–86.

2. Hautefort was completely rebuilt in the 16th, 17th, and early 19th centuries.

3. The castle of Hautefort was the scene of a number of battles, for according to his biographers, Bertran de Born "was ever at war with all his neighbors." Bertran held the family fortress in common with his brother Constantin but ousted the latter from the castle after a quarrel. Constantin appealed to Richard, their duke, to retake the castle, and in the summer of 1183 Richard's army took the fortress, but according to the *razos* Bertran was reawarded his castle by Henry II because the latter was moved by the troubadour's grief at the death of the Young King (cf. Pound's translations of "Planh for the Young English King," P, 35).

4. Cf. "Provincia Deserta": "I have looked south from Hautefort, / thinking of Montaignac, southward" (P, 126). Pound's 1912 manuscript reads Mont*i*gnac; the spellings "Montaignac" or "Montagnac" (in "Near Perigord") are clearly errors. Pound may well have been inspired by Smith's description: "Down below the towers and gates of Uzerche the dark Vézère travels thirty leagues to go twelve, and finally comes in its own way to Montignac. Thither went Bertran de Born, too, but not by a route so indolent, for at the end of the journey, in a lofty castle buttressed by a natural pillar of black ivy-wreathed stone forty feet high, and boldly over-looking the town and the

river, Lady Maeut, a sister of Maria de Ventadorn, waited to smile upon him" (II, 223).

5. Pound's Provençal is extremely corrupt, but may be roughly translated as follows: "Scarcely doth that heart of mine wilt / For the barons in their armor / And the brave men who lost their crosses / . . . / But those refined joys / and the Ladies of yesteryear / Who were so well praised / loved and unloved / As has been noted."

6. Though no scholars had mentioned Blis-et-Born in connection with the poet, Pound may have been encouraged to seek out the site of the original Born castle by a footnote in Smith: "It is stated in the books on Born that the ruins of the original Born castle may be seen, not far from Dalon, in the forest above the lake of Born and below Bellegarde, and I was determined to find them. I went within about a mile of this locality and questioned about a dozen persons. All agreed that no such ruins existed, though I was told of an old lime-kiln thereabouts. The ruins may be there, but it did not seem worth my while to prosecute the search further" (II, 428).

7. This encounter and its retelling in Canto 80 are further clarified by Pound's 1936 essay "Possibilities of Civilization: What the Small Town Can Do": "I have seen various manners in my time; the first three examples that really impressed me as perfect were those of a Russian Prince, of a Japanese Daimyo, and thirdly of a huge red-bearded peasant at Born. He was engaged in a job of amateur cobbling, mending one of his children's shoes, when I lost the road between Perigord and Excideuil and came into his cottage in search of an omelet. Gentleness and dignity" (*Impact*, 77).

8. "Lost: Small yellow dog / answers to the name *Lôve*." The resonances of the dog's name ("louve" is a she-wolf) no doubt caught Pound's ear. According to legend, the troubadour Peire Vidal, maddened by his unrequited love for the "she-wolf" Loba de Puegnautier, dressed in wolf-skins and was almost killed by hounds during a hunt. See Pound's "Piere Vidal Old" (P, 28) and Canto 4.

EXCIDEUIL

1. See Hugh Kenner, *The Pound Era*, p. 336. The phrase "Arnaut turned there" (as well as the theological angst) would appear to refer to Eliot's "Ash Wednesday." Eliot had dedicated *The Waste Land* to Pound, borrowing Dante's epithet for Arnaut Daniel, "il miglior fabbro." Pound may be returning the compliment—although Excideuil's Giraut de Borneil, the most intellectually Eliotic of all the troubadours, would seem even more apt.

2. Metonymies of memory: "Nancy" is Nancy Cunard, whose walking tours and eventual residence in the Dordogne had been inspired by Pound. The "vair and the cisclatons" are from "Troubadours: Their Sorts and Conditions" (LE, 107).

3. The turret and the windows belong to the main residence and chapel of the castle, not to its towering medieval dungeon whose parapets look out on the meadows of the river Loue.

4. May allude to the Talleyrand family, to whom Excideuil belonged from 1613 to 1883, when Hélie Roger Duc de Périgord, Prince de Chalais, Marquis d'Excideuil, willed the property to the Hospices of Chalais.

CHALUS

1. Over the course of much of the 19th century the castle of Hautefort belonged to the Baron Maxence Damas, close associate of King Charles X and governor of his son, the Duc de Bordeaux. The castle was sold in 1890 to M. Artigues, a high-ranking government engineer.

2. Pound again stayed at the Hotel Poujol in Excideuil in the summer of 1919; it is mentioned at 74/442.

3. "It will speed you on your way."

4. "Neither frost nor wind nor rain." From William IX's fifth song: *"Farai chansoneta nueva / Ans que vent ni gel ni plueva"* ("I'll make a new little song / Before the wind and the frost and the rains come").

UZERCHE AND BRIVE

1. The full proverb is "Whoever has a house at Uzerche has a castle in Limousin" (Smith II, 190)—the allusion being to the imposing turreted town-houses that sit high on the hill of Uzerche.

2. Uc Bacalairia was a minor troubadour from Labachellerie, near Périgueux; Pound quotes from the *vida* of Gaucelm Faidit (1180–1215) in "Troubadours: Their Sorts and Conditions": "Faidit, a joglar of Uzerche, 'was exceedingly greedy both to drink and to eat, and he became fat beyond measure. And he took to wife a public woman; very fair and well taught she was, but she became as big and fat as he was'" (LE, 99).

3. The 12th-century castle of Chalusset was the ancient residence of Bertran's allies, the Viscounts of Limoges; it can be seen from the railway viaduct between Limoges and Uzerche.

4. Dante Gabriel Rossetti's portrait of *Lilith* (1868) depicts a pre-Raphaelite stunner gazing at herself in a mirror as she combs out her luxurious hair.

5. According to Baedeker, Gundebald was proclaimed King of Aquitania in Brive in 585.

6. The town of Malemort-sur-Corrèze, on the outskirts of Brive, is mentioned in Canto 6 in connection with Bernart of Ventadorn's love for Eleanor of Aquitaine: "By river-marsh, by galleried church-porch, / Malemorte [*sic*], Correze." In his chapter on Uzerche, however, Smith identifies Malemort as the castle of Audiart, unhappily loved by Gaucelm Faidit (II, 22).

THE DORDOGNE

1. See Ronald Bush, *The Genesis of Ezra Pound's Cantos* (Princeton, 1976), pp. 121–22.

2. The 12th-century Romanesque parish church of Souillac contains a striking bas relief of the prophet Isaiah just inside its entranceway; Diaghilev had brought Nijinsky and the Ballets Russes to London in 1911.

3. Cf. "Provincia Deserta": "and in Sarlat, / I have climbed rickety stairs, heard talk of Croy" (P, 126). The castle of Paluel belonged to the counts of Vigier from the 12th through the 15th centuries; it was acquired by the Prince de Croy at the turn of the century.

4. Pound transcribes from his Baedeker: "Rocamadour, romantically situated in a ravine . . . is one of the most ancient pilgrim-resorts in France, especially frequented in mediaeval times. The name is derived from St. Amadour who is said to have lived here in the 1st. cent., and is identified with Zacchaeus the Publican."

5. Elias Cairal (fl. 1220–30), Aimeric de Sarlat (1190–1290), Giraut de Salignac (fl. 1200). Pound quotes from a *vida* of Cairels [*sic*] in LE, 98 ("ill he sang, ill he composed, ill he played the fiddle and worse he spoke"). He is mentioned as an example of the exhaustion of troubadour tradition at the end of Canto 6.

6. From the final section of Arnaut Daniel's *"L'aura amara"*: *"Anz vos desir / Plus que Dieus cill de Doma,"* translated by Pound as "God draws not nigh / to Dome, with pleas / Wherein's so little veering" and footnoted: "Our Lady of Puy-de-Dôme? No definite solution of this reference yet found" (LE, 129). See Makin, p. 171.

7. "Looks at and is looked at."

8. The Spanish designation for the St. John's Eve refers to Lope de Vega's midsummer night's masque, *La noche de San Juan*. St. John's Eve falls on June 23; Pound arrived at the end of the festivities, probably around July 1.

ALBI AND TOULOUSE

1. Le Sieur de Rodez is probably Enric I, Count of Rodez, subject of a *tenso* by Ugo de Sain Circ. Dante mentions Cahors (infamous in the Middle Ages as a center for usury) in *Inferno* XI, 49–51: "E però lo minor giron suggella / Del segno suo et Sodoma e Caorsa, / E chi, spregiando Dio, col cor favella." (Binyon: "The smallest ring hath therefore sealed and signed / For its own both Sodom's and Cahors' offence, / And all who speak with scorn of God in mind.")

2. St. Antonin-Noble-Val and Penne, both on the Aveyron, are no doubt associated in Pound's mind with the story of the Viscount St. Antoni and Viscount Pena that figures prominently in Ur-Canto 2. The city of Montauban, however, has nothing to do with the troubadour poet known as the Monk of Montaudon, whose priory was near Aurillac in the Auvergne.

3. "And everything that I make that is pleasing," from Peire Vidal's "Ab l'alen tir vas me l'aire."

4. *"Peire d'Alvenhe a tal votz / que chanta cum granolh' en potz"* ("Peire d'Auvergne has such a voice / that he sings like a frog in the well"), from Peire d'Auvergne's *"Chanterai d'aquestz trobadors."*

5. Mentioned in "Troubadours: Their Sorts and Conditions," LE, 99.

6. According to Baedeker, the Cathedral of St. Cecilia in Albi was begun in 1282, that is, after the apogee of the *gai savoir* (or "gay science") of the troubadours. The coastal town of Aigues-Mortes was founded in 1246 by St. Louis who used it as his point of embarkation for the crusades of 1248 and 1270.

7. The town of Albi gave its name to the sect of the Albigenses and to the war which, as Baedeker puts it, "deluged the South of France with blood from 1209 to 1229."

8. The troubadour Folquet de Marseille, apologist for Simon de Montfort's savage Albigensian Crusade, is placed into the *"cielo terzo"* of Dante's *Paradiso* (IX, 64–108) on the basis that he had been made bishop of Toulouse in 1205.

9. The Romanesque and Gothic church of Rabestans is decorated with frescoes of the 14th-15th centuries.

10. The Dante tag (*"non di più"*) refers to *Purgatorio* XXVIII, 7ff.: *"Un'aura dolce, senza mutamento / Avere in sè, mi ferìa per la fronte / Non di più colpo che soave vento"* (Binyon: "Gentle air, having no inconstancies / Within its motion, smote upon my brow / With no more violence than a gracious breeze"). The other tag (*"qu'amas l'aura"*) is Arnaut Daniel's *senhal* or punning signature, *"Ieu sui Arnautz qu'amas l'aura"* ("I am Arnaut who gathers the wind").

11. *Inferno* IX 100: *"Poi si rivolse per la strada lorda, / E non fe' motto a noi; ma fe' sembiante / D'uomo cui altra cura stringa et morda // Che quella di colui che gli è davante."* (Binyon: "Then on the unclean journey, without word / Spoken to us, returned he, and looked like one / By other business constrained and spurred / Than that of those before him.")

12. The 12th-century Romanesque church of St. Sernin has an unusual nave with double aisles; San Zeno Maggiore is a large Romanesque church in Verona, site of the signed column mentioned in the Usury Cantos.

13. La Daurade, an early Romanesque church on the quay of the Garonne, was completely rebuilt in the late 18th century. It was here, according to legend, that the Italian poet Guido Cavalcanti first met Mandetta, the mysterious *"giovane donna di Tolosa"* of his love poetry. The tag *"accordatta e stretta"* is taken from Cavalcanti's Ballata VII: *"Io dissi: E'mi ricorda ch'en Tolosa / Donna m'apparve accordellata et stretta, / La quale Amor chiamava la Mandetta . . ."* Pound's version: "Maid o' the wood, I said, my memories render / Tolosa and the dusk and these things blended: / A lady in a corded bodice, slender / —Mandetta is the name Love's spirits lend her" (T, 112–13).

14. Clemence Isaure, the 15th-century benefactress of the Académies des Jeux-Floraux, is said to be buried under the high altar of La Daurade. The flowers for successful candidates in the annual Jeux-Floraux poetry competitions are blessed in the church every May 3rd.

THE PYRENEES

1. Pound quotes the Count of Foix's Provençal text in its entirety in "Troubadours: Their Sorts and Conditions" (LE, 100) and gives the following translation: "Let no man lounge amid the flowers / Without a stout club of some kind. / Know ye the

French are stiff in stour/And sing not all they have in mind,/So trust ye not in Carcason,/In Genovese, nor in Gascon."

2. The two rivers are the Arget and the Ariège, the mountain is Mt. Pech.

3. Pound seems to be confusing this town with the Poitou home of the troubadour Savaric de Mauleon, patron of Gaubertz de Poicebot (see LE, 95 and Canto 4).

4. "O day and dazzling white gem."

5. Smith I, 368–85 contains a very good account of the Albigensians, but makes no reference to their temple stronghold at Montségur. Pound's 1877 Guide Joanne to the Pyrenees mentions it only in passing and Baedeker's 1907 guidebook to Southern France does not even note its existence. If Pound therefore did not think Montségur worth visiting in 1912, it was because it was barely on the map.

6. Those belonging to French physician and philologist Julies Caesar Scaliger (1484–1558)?

7. The celebrated defile of St. Georges, between Quillan and Axat, is described in purple prose by Smith I, 312–13. It is probably to this narrow gorge carved by the river Aude that Pound alludes in his final Pisan Canto: "and as who passed the gorges between sheer cliffs/as it might be by, is it the Garonne?/where one walks into Spagna" (84/552).

8. Smith's description of the defile of St. Georges concludes: ". . . and the mind, wearied by vain efforts to surmount the grandeur of the view, falls back upon itself, and can only repeat that sentence of the great French poet, 'L'impossible est ici debout' ('Here stands the impossible, erect on its feet'). The references to Gautier and Musset would appear to be a private joke.

9. See "Troubadours: Their Sorts and Conditions" (LE, 99).

10. In "Proença," SOR, 55.

11. Cabaret, scene of Vidal's lupine courtship of Loba de Puegnautier—see "Piere Vidal Old": "Ah! Cabaret! Ah Cabaret, thy hills again!" (CEP, 109). Smith correctly locates Cabaret near Carcassonne; Capestang, home of Guilhem de Cabestang, is near Perpignan.

THE LANGUEDOC COAST

1. The restoration and preservation of Carcassonne was undertaken by Viollet-le-Duc between 1850 and 1879. The town of Pennautier lies to the northwest of the city.

2. "For the glory of the land/To the memory/of the vicountess/Ermengard XII/and of the troubadours/Bernhart Alan/Gui. Fabre XIIIth/G. Riguier/glorious sons of/Narbonne the fertile"

3. Smith I, 219 describes Narbonne as a "dull provincial town."

4. Latin name for the Roman province of which Narbo was the capital. *Aymeri de Narbonne* is the early 13th-century *chanson de geste* associated with the city.

5. Home of the troubadour Guilhem de Cabestang whose heart was served as a meal by Raimon, Lord of Rousillon, to his unfaithful wife Soremonde. Smith I, 238. See Canto 4.

6. "A guisa de leon . . . quando si posa" ("As a lion does . . . when he rests"), *Purgatorio* VI, 66, describing Sordello.

7. The river Aude marks the boundary between the provinces of Aude and Hérault.

8. Tiborc (or Guiborc) of Montausier was the vicountess of Chalais mentioned in Bertran's *"Dompna pois de me no'us chal."*

9. Béziers and its viscount play a prominent role in Pound's early poem "Marvoil" (P, 21).

10. I.e. the Roman poet Horace.

11. Title of Baudelaire's prose poem "Enivrez-vous."

12. Pound lived in Venice in 1908 and spent the spring of 1910 and 1911 in Sirmio.

ARLES, NÎMES, AND BEAUCAIRE

1. The kingdom of Arles was part of the Holy Roman Empire, ruled by Frederick Barbarossa from 1155 to 1190; it is uncertain whether Dante ever visited Arles.

2. *Inferno* IX, 112, describing the City of Dis: *"Sì com ad Arli, ove il Rodano stagna"* (Binyon: "Like as at Arles, where Rhone stagnates in sand, / Like as at Pola, by Quarnaro Sound, / That barriers Italy and bathes her strand, / Sepulchres make uneven all the ground, / So here on every side were tombs arrayed, / Only that here was the bitterer burial found.")

3. *Inferno* X, 52–54, describing the shade of Calvalcante de' Cavalcanti, father of Guido: *"Allor surse alla vista scoperchiata / Un'ombra lungo questo infino al mento; / Credo che s'era in ginocchie levata."* (Binyon: "Beside him then a shadow by degrees / Emerged, and was discovered to the chin: / I think he had raised himself upon his knees.")

4. Pound's observations of the lidless stone sarcophagi lining the tree-shaded alley of the Aliscamps (which resemble troughs with semicircular lunules or "head holes" cut out on the side) presumably gloss Dante's descriptions of the tombs opening in the City of Dis in *Inferno*, IX, 121–123: *"Tutti gli lor coperchi eran sospesi; / E furor n'uscivan si duri lamenti, / Che ben parean di miseri e d'offesi."* (Binyon: "Their covers were all raised up in our view, / And out of them such harsh lamenting rose / As from a wretched and a wounded crew."). In *The Pound Era* (p. 477), Kenner argues that Pound later remembers these open trough-like tombs as Confucian "rain altars" in The Pisan Cantos: "as he had walked under the rain altars / or under the trees of their grove / or would it be under their parapets / in his moving was stillness / as grey stone in the Aliscans" (80/526). The Dante tag, "si com ad Arli," reoccurs in the same Canto.

5. I.e. "walk" or "promenade." Pound's spelling of the word conflates the Spanish (*"paseo"*) with the Portuguese (*"passeio"*).

6. This entire Arles section is written on local Hôtel du Forum stationery, decorated with the image of a bee and the Félibrige poet Frédéric Mistral's Provençal motto *"lou soleu me fai cantar"* ("the sun makes me sing").

7. The "other school," as "Psychology and Troubadours" makes clear, is that of the intellectual *trobar clus*, as opposed to the more populist tradition of the "ballad-concert" (SOR, 88).

8. Cf. the spring festival dances that Pound describes in "Proença": "But we are

hardly fair in comparing *La Régine Avrillouse* to the Latin verse, which follows the classic dance of worship. Our quasi-Zarabondilla, or Tarantella, is the successor, one supposes, of the Cordax of the later Empire" (SOR, 40).

9. In the 1917 Ur-Canto 1, the Arles arena provides the theater for the visions Pound sets against those of Browning's *Sordello*: "Or shall I do your trick, the show-man's booth, Bob Browning, / Turned at my will into the Agora, / Or into the old theatre at Arles, / And set the lot, my visions, to confounding / The wits that have survived your damn'd *Sordello?*" (P, 232) The tiered arena of vision (now probably Verona's) returns at 21/98: "and we sit here / By the arena, *les gradins* . . ."

10. Root ideogram of Cantos 2–6, which overlay Hellas, China and Japan, and Provence.

11. Cf. Pound's discussion of the different "phases of consciousness" in "I Gather the Limbs of Osiris" (SP, 29–30).

12. Beaucaire derives etymolgically from the Latin Bellum Quadrum (Baedeker). Pound mentions the tower of Beaucaire at 76/469 ("and the tower on an almost triangular base / as seen from Santa Marta's in Tarascon") and at 96/673.

13. A stronghold of the Languedoc rebels leagued against Louis XIII, Beaucaire was destroyed by Richelieu in 1632.

THE AUVERGNE

1. Smith devotes a chapter to Le Puy and its poet Peire Cardinal (II, 31–38). Pound discusses Peire Cardinal's importance as a satirist at length in "Troubadours—Their Sorts and Conditions" (LE, 104–07).

2. The Cathedral of Notre-Dame (11th–12th cents.) is noted for its unusual mixture of bands of white and black stone.

3. The Church of St. Michel d'Aiguilhe in Le Puy takes its name from the needle of rock on which it is perched.

4. In his chapter devoted to the town of Polignac, near Le Puy, Smith discusses the loves of Guilhem de Sain Leidier (or Saint-Didier) at length (II, 48–62). "Polonhoc" is mentioned in the Cantos (4/16), Pound having confused the viscount of Polignac with Raimon de Castel-Roussillon who had Guillem de Cabestan's heart served up for dinner.

5. Pound mentions local troubadour Peire d'Auvergne's song to the nightingale ("*Rossinhol al seu repaire*") in "Proença" (SOR, 49).

6. The Benedictine abbey of Chaise-Dieu ("Casa Dei") was founded in 1043 by St. Robert. Pope Clement VI, who was originally one of its monks, lies buried in the abbey church. The church also contains an array of Flemish tapestries from the early 16th century which represent allegorical scenes from the Bible. Perhaps inspired by his rereading of his walking tour notes, Pound remembered these tapestries at the end of *Thrones*: "The tapestries were still there in Chaise Dieu, / The sky's glass leaded with elm boughs" (107/775).

7. Stefano di Givanni da Verona (1375–1438?), painter of the Madonna del Roseta (Madonna of the Rose Garden); mentioned at 4/16.

FRAGMENTS FROM *GIRONDE*

1. Pound quotes Peire Vidal's "Song of Breath" in "Proença" (SOR, 49): "*Ab l'alen tir vas me l'aire / Qu'eu sen venir de Provensa / Tot quant es de lai m'agensa / Si que quan n'aug ben retraire / Eu m'o escut en rizen / E'n deman per un mot cen / Tan m'es bels quan n'aug ben dire.*" (Pound's 1910 translation: "Breathing I draw the air to me / Which I feel coming from Provença, / All that is thence so pleasureth me / That whenever I hear good speech of it / I listen laughing and straightway / Demand for each word an hundred / So fair to me is the hearing").

2. Possible allusion to the rhyme schemes Pound used in his 1911 versions of Arnaut Daniel. Cf. "Ere the Winter," LE, 142.

3. George Gascoigne's *Certayne Notes of Instruction* (1575) was the first English essay on prosody.

4. "Red Rose, proud Rose, sad Rose of all my days! / Come near me, while I sing the ancient ways," from Yeats's "To the Rose upon the Rood of Time," in *The Rose* (1893).

5. Maurice Hewlett's 1912 "Lai of Gaubertz" imitates the virtuoso triple rhymes of the troubadours (aaabaaab, cccdcccd, etc.). In his May 1913 *Poetry* review of Hewlett's *Helen Redeemed and Other Poems*, Pound observed: "His chief interest from the technical point of view lies in his skillful use of harsh rime to check the verse suddenly and to keep it in swift motion, a system of barring which is efficient in a manner similar to the Anglo-Saxon alliterative devices."

6. Pound's translation of Arnaut Daniel's "*Autet e bas,*" first published in "I Gather the Limbs of Osiris" (*The New Age*, 11 Jan. 1912), is reprinted in LE, 124–27. Each stanza of the poem is punctuated by variations on the sound of a bird call ("*Cadahus / En son us*")—variously rendered by Pound as "Letteth loose / Wriblis spruce," "They reduce / Pains, and noose," "Word's abuse / Doth traduce," etc.

7. Robert Southey (1774–1843), named Poet Laureate in 1813; Sir Lewis Morris (1833–1907), minor English poet.

8. Pound began working on his projected edition of Arnaut Daniel at the Bibliothèque Nationale in the spring of 1911. He subsequently traveled to Milan in late July to consult Ms. R71 superiore at the Ambrosian Library—the sole manuscript containing the musical notation for two of Arnaut Daniel's poems ("*Chansson doil mot*" and "*Lo ferm voler*").

9. Pound worked on musical settings of troubadour poetry with the composer Walter Morse Rummel in Paris over the course of the spring and summer 1912. The 1912 preface to *Hesternae Rosae, Serta II* (1913), a collection of Rummel's settings of Pound's English versions of nine troubadour songs (including the two Arnaut Daniel melodies from the Ambrosian Library) reads: "The writer with the help of Mr. Ezra Pound, an ardent proclaimer of the artistic side of mediaeval poetry, has given these melodies the rhythm and the ligature, the character which, from an artistic point of view, seems the most descriptive of the mediaeval spirit." During the spring and summer of 1912 Pound also worked on troubadour manuscripts at the Bibliothèque Nationale. A small notebook among the *Walking Tour* papers at Beinecke contains numerical references to following manuscripts: 844, 852, 854[I], 856, 858, 1749[E], 20050, 12473[K], 22543[R].

10. Bibliothèque Nationale Ms. Fr. 844 (known as the "Chansonnier du Roi") is evoked in Ur-Canto 2 à propos of two lines of music by "Joios, Tolosan" that Pound had transcribed in 1912: "There's the one stave, and all the rest forgotten. / I've lost the copy I had of it in Paris, / Out of the blue and gilded manuscript / Decked out with Couci's rabbits, / And the pictures, twined with the capitals, / Purporting to be Arnaut's and the authors." Several lines later Pound goes on to evoke Ms. R71 superiore at the Ambrosian Library: "Or there's En Arnaut's score of songs, two tunes" (P, 235). The particular configuration of the capitals in Ms. Fr. 844 strikingly foreshadows Henry Strater's initials for the deluxe 1925 edition of *A Draft of XVI Cantos*.

11. Ms. fr. 854, also known as siglum I, is the source for most of the *vidas* and *razos* included in Pound's 1913 "Troubadours: Their Sorts and Conditions" (although, judging from his manuscript notes, he may have also consulted E, K, and R): "Or he may learn the outlines of these events from the 'razos,' or prose paragraphs of introduction, which are sometimes called 'lives of the troubadours.' And, if he have mind for these latter, he will find in the Bibliothèque Nationale at Paris the manuscript of Miquel de la Tour, written perhaps in the author's own handwriting; at least we read 'I, Miquel de la Tour, scryven, do ye to wit'" (LE, 95). Ms. fr. 854, which contains eighty-five troubadour biographies, dates from the 13th century and is in an Italian hand. The identification "Et ieu, maistre Miquel de la Tor, escrivan," appears only in the vida of Peire Cardinal; the authorship of the remainder of the biographies is uncertain. See Jean Boutière and A.-J. Schutz, *Biographies des Troubadours* (Toulouse, 1950).

12. The remainder of the typescript consists of cut-up snippets of twenty-one troubadour *vidas* and *razos*—in all likelihood the textual debris left over from the series of biographical summaries that were recycled into the published version of "Troubadours: Their Sorts and Conditions."